LONDON – VENICE – DUBROV

A Journey into the Levant as It Once Was

John & Renata Fox

Cover illustration: A sixteenth century painting of a Ragusan argosy that belonged to the aristocratic family of Ohmučević, who fled from Bosnia during the Ottoman conquest of the Balkans in 1463. Source: Franciscan Church, Slano, Croatia.

First published 2019
by Rowanvale Books Ltd
The Gate
Keppoch Street
Roath
Cardiff
CF24 3JW
www.rowanvalebooks.com

A CIP catalogue record for this book is available from the British Library.
ISBN: 978-1-912655-23-6

We wish to thank the following institutions, organisations and persons for their valuable knowledge and kind help: Archaeological Museum of Istria, Blue Water Holidays, British Library, Franciscan Church, Slano, Götzfried Antique Maps, Harvard Art Museums, Croatian Conservation Institute, David Rumsey Historical Map Collection, Dubrovnik State Archives, Dubrovnik Tourist Board, Istanbul University, Lausanne Shoe Museum, Switzerland, National Portrait Gallery, Paulus Swaen Old Maps & Prints, Royal Society, Sailgreece.net, Stari Grad Museum, Hvar, Town Museum, Korčula, Villas Croatia.

ABOUT THE AUTHORS

John and Renata Fox live on the Adriatic coast. John spends his time looking at the sea. Renata grows flowers and cooks. John and Renata have followed the British gentleman wherever he went. Like he, they write for all who wish to learn.

For our son Ivan

CONTENTS

INTRODUCTION

And one mile beyond that is a stone marking the boundaries of the Venetian and Turkish dominions. We were no sooner past it but we entered into Christendom which seemed to us altogether a new world, such was the alteration we found not only in the inhabitants but also in the soil. Here the fields are well manured and in the midst of corn-fields, olives, pomegranates, pines and figs.

> *- Peter Mundy crossing the Balkan Peninsula on his way home from Constantinople in 1620.*

What a captivating experience it must have been to make a journey into the Levant when so little was known about other people. But Peter Mundy's description of what he saw is much more than just a window into a vanished world: think of the stone not only as a marker of "the boundaries of the Venetian and Turkish dominions", but also as standing for the centuries of historical processes that had created the cultural divide. For Peter Mundy, this was knowledge worthy to be learned. It was the Early Modern Age, and at last, "miracles were past".

Based on the British gentleman's travelogue, this book takes you, too, on a journey into the Levant, as it once was, and it aims to explain that world. Who was the British gentleman, and why did he write about his travels abroad? Why was the Levant so important to him, and how did he reach it? What did he think of the famous cities he visited and the people he met?

The book is about travel when London was at the very best two months away from Constantinople, about a traveller who did not always return home and about the ways of people of long ago.

PETER MUNDY (1600-1667) was the son of a Cornwall merchant family that exported pilchards to France and Spain.

After spending much of his life travelling abroad, in around 1647, he finally settled down and married. He wrote his travelogue, he explains, "to pleasure such friends that are desirous to understand somewhat of foreign countries". Peter Mundy never printed his travelogue. In the Early Modern Age, manuscript culture was still very strong, and it was quite common for the British gentleman to circulate his writings through a network of friends.

THE BRITISH GENTLEMAN

When, in the thirteenth century, King Edward I commissioned the sons of the dukes, barons and knights of England to serve as crown administrators, he created as well a new social group, popularly called "gentlemen", from the Latin word *gentilis*, meaning belonging to the same family.

The gentleman quickly became an established member of society. In 1363, "gentleman" was included in the Sumptuary Laws of England that regulated what certain people could wear, eat and buy according to their social status. In 1413, "gentleman" was added to the Statute of Additions that standardised designations in legal documents, e.g. wills and writs. And "gentleman" had entered literature, too: "To do whatever noble deeds he can, And take him for the greatest gentleman", wrote the great English poet Geoffrey Chaucer in 1386 in his *The Canterbury Tales*.

By the Early Modern Age, "gentleman" was a word rich in meanings. It referred to a particular social group of men with particular obligations and behaviours – including why and how the gentleman should travel abroad:

> For if you should travel but to travel, or to say you had travelled, certainly you should prove a pilgrim, no more. But I presume so well of you (that though a great number of us never thought in ourselves why we went, but a certain tickling humour to do as other men had done) your purpose, being a Gentleman born, to furnish yourself with the knowledge of such things as may be serviceable for your country & calling. Which certainly stands not in the change of air (for the warmest sun makes not a wise man) no, nor in learning languages (although they be of serviceable use) for words are but words in what language so ever they be.
>
> *- Sir Philip Sidney's letter to his younger brother Robert, the first Earl of Leicester, who had sought his advice on travel abroad, dated 1580.*

The gentleman born was well off, educated and he possessed a coat of arms.

Fig. 1. The Sidneys' coat of arms with the motto *"Quo fata vocant"*, wherever fate summons me. Source: Swyrich Corporation. Dating back to the thirteenth century and a John de Sydenie, a Surrey yeoman from the parish of Alford, the Sidneys' lineage was well defined. On the father's side, the Sidneys had for generations been personal servants to the kings of England; on the mother's side, since time immemorial, the Dudleys were nobility.

But England was changing. The growing populations needed more food; the new industries, more workers; and a booming trade, more administration. The upshot was an increasingly integrated society with a new social order. The landlord and the peasant were replaced by the property owner and the labourer. The master craftsmen united into powerful guilds to regulate training, labour, quality and wages. And the industrialists, merchants, bankers and lawyers became immensely influential. At the end of the seventeenth century, to paraphrase Daniel Defoe's satirical poem *The True-Born Englishman*, "Antiquity and birth were needless in England; 'Twas impudence and money made a peer". The gentleman born was now joined by the gentleman made.

SIR PHILIP SIDNEY (1554-1586) – "the flower of English manhood" – lived only until the age of thirty-one. Shot in the thigh at the Battle of Zutphen and lying fatally wounded on the battlefield, he offered his water bottle to another wounded soldier saying: "Thy necessity is yet greater than mine". He was buried in St Paul's Cathedral, London. His funeral was of the splendour of kings and queens.

Sir Philip Sidney's letter to his brother was published in 1633 in *Profitable Instructions describing what special observations are to be taken by travellers in all nations, states and countries; pleasant and profitable. By the three much admired, Robert, late Earle of Essex. Sir Philip Sidney. And, Secretary Davison.* The publication is an example of the *ars apodemica*: advice literature on the many aspects of travel abroad at that time.

KNOWLEDGE

In 1553, on his way to see Jerusalem, aboard a Venetian galley some fifty miles off the port of Jaffa, Michael John Lok watched the rescue of the "ship's cat":

> It chanced by fortune that the ship's cat leaped into the sea, which being down, kept her self very valiantly above water, notwithstanding the great waves, still swimming, that which the master knowing, he caused the skiff with half a dozen men to go towards her and fetch her again, when she was almost half a mile from the ship, and all this while the ship lay on stays. I hardly believe they would have made such haste and means if one of the company had been in the like peril.

He wrote about it, he further explains, "to note the estimation that cats are in, among the Italians, for generally they esteem their cats as in England we esteem a good Spaniel".

For Michael John Lok – as for many other young British gentlemen who, at that time, also travelled abroad to see the famous cities – the ways of other people were there to be observed, described and explained. They stood for a new, exciting understanding of knowledge, which had emerged in the Early Modern Age.

Not that such cultural knowledge was previously entirely unknown. The Greeks had also studied the world around them. Solon, wrote Plutarch in his *Parallel Lives*, spent ten years journeying through Egypt, Cyprus and Asia Minor to learn about foreign governments and laws. To compile his *History*, Herodotus travelled through Greece and Egypt: "the timeless gift of the Nile, the land of sphinx and pyramid, of bright sun beating down overhead and dusty earth underfoot", as he saw this land, as well as Asia Minor and Mesopotamia. And in his *Lives of Eminent Philosophers*, the Greek biographer Diogenes Laertius told of how Plato visited Euclid in Megara, Theodorus Mathematicus in Cyrene and the Pythagorean philosophers in Italy. What happened was that, with the fall of the Roman Empire in the fifth century, Europe lost touch with its Greek philosophical and scientific roots.

The return to knowledge began at the beginning of the ninth century. It was the product of Charlemagne, or rather Charles the Great, who, inspired by the Christian Roman Empire, began what today is known as the Carolingian Renaissance. It was, too, under Charlemagne that feudalism and the manorial system developed.

By the twelfth century, scholars such as Gerard of Cremona were translating Greek and Arabic texts into Latin. The works of Aristotle, Euclid, Ptolemy, Archimedes and Galen were studied at the great Italian universities of Salerno and Bologna. In addition, an alternative philosophy called scholasticism, which sought to harmonise Christian theology with classical and late antiquity philosophy through dialectical reasoning and inference, had developed. At this time, too, the magnificent Gothic-style cathedrals of Paris, Reims, York and Cologne were built.

And when, in the fourteenth century, based on their study of the "lost literature", Petrarch and Boccaccio offered an understanding of life founded on intellectual freedom and individual expression, the way ahead towards the triumph of knowledge was laid.

Humanism, as this new understanding was named, changed the world. It gave the Italian Renaissance, which spread throughout the whole of Europe. If, before, a king's fame had been measured through his success at war, now it was the palaces and the artists and scholars at his court that counted. A famous Renaissance city was Florence, home to Leonardo da Vinci, Botticelli, Michelangelo and Dante. Its rulers, the Medicis, spent enormous sums of money on encouraging art and science.

But for knowledge to freely spread, it had to become independent and available to all. The invention of the printing press by the German Johann Guttenberg in 1448 enabled this. Indeed, without print, the Protestant Reformation would not have succeeded as it did. When on 31 October 1517 Martin Luther posted his ninety-five theses, just two weeks were needed for their distribution throughout Germany, and one month throughout Europe. He referred to print as "God's highest act of grace".

And, of course, there were the magnificent voyages of discovery that made available new knowledge of other lands. In 1488, Bartholomew Diaz sailed around the Cape of Good Hope. In 1492, Christopher Columbus discovered America. In 1519, Ferdinand Magellan started the first circumnavigation of the globe.

***

In England, the Renaissance started much later than on the Continent. Not until 1476 did the country get its first printing press, set up by William Claxton. The great churches and civic buildings of Inigo Jones and Sir Christopher Wren were built in the seventeenth century, and landscape painting, which embodied a new perspective on life and elsewhere was well established as a genre, did not appear until the eighteenth century. For such reasons, the English Renaissance has been called the English Reformation. It began in the sixteenth century during the reign of Henry VIII, took off under Queen Elizabeth I, and it lasted until 1685 and the end of the reign of Charles II, who re-established the Church of England and wiped out the religious tolerance of Cromwell's days. The energies created by the inseparability of the secular and the religious during this time made England great.

On 26 September 1580, Francis Drake arrived in Plymouth with his ship the *Golden Hind*. He had circumnavigated the globe and brought home a cargo of gold. By the beginning of the seventeenth century, Shakespeare had taken literary achievement to the highest order. And in 1605, in his *The Advancement of Learning*, Sir Francis Bacon set the foundation for modern scientific inquiry based on what he called the "mechanical arts": human activities that accomplished things that nature could not. Three technological discoveries, he maintained, had changed man's ability to control the natural world: printing, gunpowder and the magnet. Voltaire would later add the invention of glass.

As the importance of knowledge to society grew, so new understandings of it were given. In its first issue of *The Philosophical Transactions*, dated 6 March 1665, the Royal Society defined knowledge as that which excluded "all Discourse of Divinity, of State-Affairs, and of News".

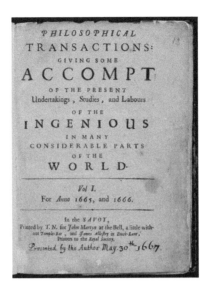

Fig. 2. The title page of *The Philosophical Transactions of the Royal Society*. Source: Royal Society. This esteemed publication did more than publish knowledge. It brought together scientists and created a scientific atmosphere and a sense of competition amongst them; it established what today we would call a scientific discourse community.

In 1687, in his *Mathematical Principles of Natural Philosophy*, Sir Isaac Newton saw knowledge as establishing the laws of nature. And in 1690, in his *An Essay Concerning Human Understanding*, the renowned English philosopher John Locke offered a more philosophical understanding of knowledge. The substance of knowledge, he said, were ideas that came from experience consisting of sensation of the external world. One good way to acquire ideas was to travel abroad.

MICHAEL JOHN LOK (1532-1621) was the son of Sir William Lok, a London dealer in textiles. At the age of thirteen, he was sent to Flanders and France "to learn the business of a merchant and the foreign languages" and later to Spain and Portugal where he was involved in the trade of the Spanish West Indies (Caribbean) and the East Indies (islands of Southeast Asia). Needless to say, his living abroad shaped his understanding of knowledge.

Today, Michael John Lok is usually remembered for his

association with the explorer Martin Frobisher and the financial support he gave him to find the fabled Northwest Passage to China. He was also associated with the Levant Company and from 1592 spent two years in Aleppo as the English consul. He married twice. His first wife, Joan, left him with eight children. His second wife, Mary, bore him seven children.

THE LEVANT

For most of us today, the word Levant brings to mind all of those meanings associated with that part of the world throughout history: a place where the first cultures and civilisations evolved; where the first farms, craft specialisation and long-distance trade developed; where the first cities and states were established; and where Judaism, Christianity and Islam were born. For the British gentleman of the Early Modern Age, this was not necessarily so – the Levant was a place to learn about the Turks and to establish trade.

Fig. 3. A portrait of Sir Henry Blount (1602-1682) – "the great traveller". Author unknown. Source: Claudia Hill @ Ellison Fine Art. "I was of the opinion, that he who would behold these times in their greatest glory, could not find a better scene than Turkey".

Indeed, since the reign of Henry VII (1485-1509) – "the merchant king" – the Levant had always been about trade, as the ledger books of Sir William Locke, mercer of London, dated 1511, show:

> Diverse tall ships of London with certain other ships of Southampton and Bristol, had an ordinary and usual trade to Sicily, Crete, Chios, and sometimes to Cyprus, as also to Tripoli and Beirut. The commodities they carried thither were fine kersies of diverse colours, course kersies, white western dozens, cottons, certain clothes called statutes, and others called cardinal whites, and cauleskins which were well sold in Sicily, &c. The commodities which they returned back were silks, camlets, rhubarb, malvasia, muscatels and other wines, sweet oils, cotton wool, Turkey carpets, pepper, cinnamon, and some other spices.

It was in fact the London merchants who, in need of a word for places east of Venice from where the sun rises, coined the word "Levant", from the Italian *Levante*, meaning "rising".

But England's prosperity was at its end. The reign of Henry VIII (1509-1547) was more about wives and wars. Only trade with the Baltics, from where came the products for building ships, such as flax, hemp, canvas, cordage, pitch, tar, timber and iron, survived. The agony, which included the disastrous reigns of Edward VI, the "boy king", and Mary I, "Bloody Mary", lasted until 1558 when Elizabeth I became Queen of England. Finally, as the saying went, the country had a queen who would "play the king better than any man".

In 1581, owing much to the tireless efforts of the London merchant William Harborne, the London Turkey Company, or later the Levant Company, was formed. The company exported cloth, pewter, tin for guns and lead for bullets, and imported cotton cloth, cotton wool, yarn, wool, carpets, soda ash, medicinal drugs, raw silk, currants, spices and even leather dog collars. It did not see itself as controlled by Pope Pius V's edict in his *Regnans in Excelsis*, the Bull of Deposition, dated 1570, banning trade to the "infidels", especially as he had excommunicated Elizabeth I as "a heretic and favourer of heretics".

The Levant Company had its headquarters in Aleppo (northern Syria, which in 1516 became a part of the Ottoman empire) with offices in Constantinople, Alexandria and Smyrna, and was in charge of the English consulates and embassy. It always welcomed the British gentleman when he was travelling abroad. It changed his letters of credit and provided him with accommodation and assistance. It made his journey into the Levant much easier.

***

The English never feared or hated the Turks, or used them as a scapegoat for taxes. Instead, in England, the Turks were seen as a cultural other who, if they disliked their wives, sold them in markets, so it was said.

The Turks had an enviously huge empire that spread from Budapest to Basra, from the Crimea to Cairo, from Algiers to Arabia, and was greatly admired. In the words of Sir Philip Sidney, "the Turks' discipline in war matters was, *propter se*, worthy to be learned".

Books were written about the Turks, such as Richard Knolles' *The Generall Historie of the Turkes*. The Turks were present in English theatres, too. Shakespeare's *Othello* and the *Merchant of Venice*, Philip Marlow's *Tamburlaine the Great* and *The Jew of Malta*, Robert Daborne's *Christian Turn'd Turke* and John Fletcher's *The Knight of Malta* all relied upon Turkish characters and scenes. And, of course, everybody wished to read Sir Henry Blount's fascinating stories about his journey into the Levant which he had made in 1634:

> Upon the taking of any town, the first thing they [the Turks] erect, is public baths, which they establish with fair revenues, so that for less than two pence, any man, or woman may be bathed with clean linen, and never attendant; it is death for any man to enter when women *bath,* which he shall know by a bar before the door: he or she who bath not twice, or thrice a week are held nasty.

Thieves are impaled without delay, or mercy; and there was a Saniak-bey [a high ranking officer] with two hundred horse, who did nothing but coast up, and down the country, and every man who could not give a fair account of his being where he found him, was presently strangled, though not known to have offended: for their justice although not so rash as we suppose, yet will rather cut off two innocent men, than let one offender escape.

Also, the Turkish habit of drinking coffee was beginning to be seen in London, and in 1649, the Quran was translated into English.

Yet the Ottomans had seen their heyday. *Venimus, Vidimus, Deus Vicit* – We came, We saw, God conquered – were the triumphant words of the Polish King Jan III Sobieski who in 1683 at the battle of Kahlenberg, Austria, completely destroyed the Ottoman forces. He freed Hungary, Transylvania, Slavonia, Dalmatia (today a part of Croatia) and Podolia (today a region in Ukraine).

Defeated and shamed, in the eyes of a decentralised eighteenth century Europe focused on liberty and innovation, the Turks were an inferior people. For Voltaire in his *Fanaticism, or Mahomet the Prophet* they were fanatics; for Montesquieu in his *The Spirit of the Laws* they were despots. Along with Persia and India, Turkey belonged to an undifferentiated area called the Orient. It had become what, in the nineteenth century, Nicholas I of Russia would call the "sick man of Europe".

SIR HENRY BLOUNT (1602-1682) was the third son of Sir Thomas Pope Blount of Tyttenhanger in Hertfordshire. He was knighted by Charles I in 1639. After the English Civil War, Sir Henry was employed by Oliver Cromwell to consider the ways and means to "better the trade and navigation of the Commonwealth", especially the coffee market. He was always closely connected to the Levant Company and was known to drink only coffee and water in his old age. His travelogue *A Voyage into the Levant* was first published in 1638 and was reprinted many times.

THE TRAVELOGUE

In the Early Modern Age, the young British gentleman was expected to be productively employed when travelling abroad. "It is good that you make a book of paper wherein you may daily or at least weekly insert all things occurring to you", advised William Cecil (Lord Burghley) in a letter he wrote to Edward Manners, concerning his stay in France in 1570. Such advice was also given by Sir Philip Sidney to his brother: "Your purpose, being a Gentleman born, is to furnish yourself with the knowledge of such things as may be serviceable for your Country & calling". And what better proof of this than a *peregrinationis historia*: "a true report by a skilful traveller"?

But probably the main reason why the British gentleman wrote about his travels abroad was his wish to participate in the social accumulation of knowledge, which had become so important in the Early Modern Age. In the words of Fynes Moryson, who spent years away from home, the British gentleman wrote "for all who wished to see foreign lands".

As all travel writing, the *peregrinationis historia* was the product of a particular society and culture. It was, for example, different to medieval travel writing which had often used fiction and fantasy handed down and copied from classical authors.

Fig. 4. Creatures encountered by Sir John Mandeville: a cynocephales with a "hound's head" and "an ox of gold or of silver in his forehead", a

cockodrill that has "four feet and short thighs, and great nails as claws", and "wild geese that have two heads". Source: *The Travels of Sir John Mandeville*. Written in French in 1356, *The Travels of Sir John Mandeville* was one of the first books printed and it was immensely popular.

Similarly, medieval travel writing was different to that of the ancient Greeks. Homer's Odyssey is much more than a *nostos*: a tale of difficulties experienced by heroes on their return home from exploits in foreign lands. It is as well about people and their relationships, such as Penelope's (and Argos') loyalty to Odysseus.

The Early Modern Age paved, too, the path for today's wide use of humour in society. This was a product of what the Russian philosopher Mikhail Bakhtin, in his *Rabelais and His World* (1965), called "carnivalesque": the impulse within Renaissance cultures to overthrow the established order, albeit temporarily, as happens in traditional forms of carnival. As humour became more democratic, especially through comedy in the theatre, so it found its way into the British gentleman's travelogue, although obviously in a very limited way:

A British gentleman who was staying in a German inn complained to the maid that his eggs at breakfast were (boiled) too hard. "I'd done 'em for an hour, but in the future I'll do 'em for two", she replied.

- *Fynes Moryson, Germany, 1595.*

A young, lusty, woman hard by my elbow, busy at her beads, who with the heat of the throng, and for lack of air, fell straight in a sound: the women about her gave a shout and cried out that our Blessed Lady had appeared to her; whereupon she was carried forth and laid upon the steps that descend from the chapel to the church floor, five hundredth more came to visit her with salutations of Saint, Saint, O ever Blessed Saint; Now, it was Friday morning, and the woman having travelled all night, and to save charges of fish, had eaten a cold bit of her own meat privately in the tavern with half a bucale [pitcher] of red wine. The people more admiring this imaginary trance, than the relief of the woman; I said to brother Arthur, I will go open the woman's breast, and I did so: and holding up her head before all the people, there sprung a flood of wine garbo down the alabaster stairs intermingled with lumps of ill-chewed flesh. Whereat the people being amazed, from a saint swore she was a devil. And if my friend and I had not made haste to carry the sick woman from the church to a tavern, doubtless, they would have stoned her to death.

- *William Lithgow, The Basilica of the Holy House, Loreto, Italy, 1609.*

In the Middle Ages, humour was understood as malicious; it was generally maintained that it was wrong to laugh at other people. Although Aristotle had considered wit a valuable part of conversation, he also agreed that laughter expressed scorn. Wit, he argued, was "educated insolence".

By the eighteenth century, the development of literacy, the explosion of the printing culture and the rise of individualism had given the novel. Under the influence of this new genre that focused on theme and character development, travel writing was redefined. Soon, anybody who was anybody among writers wrote at least one travel book: James Boswell – *Journal of a Tour to the Hebrides*, Henry Fielding – *Voyage to Lisbon,* Samuel Johnson – *A Journey to the Western Islands of Scotland*, Tobias Smollett – *The Expedition of Humphry Clinker* and Laurence Sterne – *A Sentimental Journey*.

And yet again, travel writing would change. Towards the end of the eighteenth century, the industrial revolution and the scientific rationalisation of life created a reaction called Romanticism. It emphasised emotions and an admiration for nature's beauty:

I know not whether you have ever seen the sun rise and set at sea; if so, you have beholden the finest object of sight to the greatest advantage. I have twice in my late voyage remained all night upon deck with the man at the helm; and, when I had watched the dawn and increasing day, was lost in admiration to view the Great Dispenser of light and heat rise from his chambers in the East and set all the water as it were in a blaze. Or in the evening, when sinking in the nether hemisphere with milder, though undiminished beams, show us, like a cloud, the distant shores of Italy.

- Thomas Watkins, the East Adriatic, 1788.

This was the time, too, when Mariana Starke (1761-1838) wrote the first travel guide for the growing number of people who began to travel abroad.

FYNES MORYSON (1566-1630) was the oldest son of a London merchant. He was educated at Peterhouse, Cambridge, and it was during his legal studies, he writes, that he began his extensive travels abroad:

From my tender youth I had a great desire to see foreign Countries, not to get liberty (which I had in Cambridge in such measure, as I could not well desire it more), but to enable my understanding which I thought could not be done so well by contemplation as by experience; nor by the ear or any sense or so well as by the eyes.

As was often the practice in those days, to cover the money he borrowed to pay for his journey into the Levant, Fynes Moryson bet with friends "one hundred pounds to receive three hundred" against his return. As the bet was not paid, he was forced to declare bankruptcy.

At first, Fynes Moryson wrote his travelogue *An Itinerary* in Latin, which at the beginning of the seventeenth century was the *lingua franca* of educated Europe. Today, *An Itinerary* is a standard reference for learning about travel abroad in the Early Modern Age.

WILLIAM LITHGOW (1582-1645) was born in Lanark, Scotland. He travelled abroad because he chose to "seclude" himself from his "soil during these modern and dissolute times". Perhaps, though, the real reason why he left Scotland was because he was caught *in flagrante* with a certain Miss Lockhart whose brothers then cut off his ears, and which later earned him the nickname "cutlugged Willie". In Rome, William almost lost his life, narrowly escaping from the Inquisition. In Spain, suspected of being an English spy, he was imprisoned and horribly tortured. Reprinted many times, William Lithgow's *Rare Adventures and Painful Peregrinations* has been described as one of the world's great travel tales.

ROUTES

To reach Constantinople from London, the British gentleman travelled along an urban network of cities, towns and villages. A city, as Peter Mundy saw when he visited Venice in 1620 on his way home from the Levant, was a place of specialisation of skills, social categories, markets and institutions and factories:

> I went with a friend to see the famous Arsenal, a place about two miles in compass, walled around and with but one entrance for a galley to go in and out although there is space for two or three hundred to ride afloat. There are about a hundred great rooms open at either end for building new vessels and some were on the stocks. From thence to the place where they cast ordnance and to the great storehouse full of ordnance ready mounted on carriages. We were shown where they made anchors, cables, ropes, oars, rudders, masts, etc. Then we went upstairs where were halls hung with armour, swords, muskets, pikes and targets. In other halls were new sails readymade which are sewn by women. In this Arsenal there dwell only the keepers; the workmen come in the morning and depart at night.

Differently, a village, as he also saw when he crossed the Balkans, was an intimate place of equals engaged in shared responsibilities and activities:

> At our passage through any village they would stand ready with hot cakes. Also milk, sweet and sour, fresh cheese, butter and eggs, being brought to us by the youngest and prettiest wenches, and these, with the young women, holding hand in hand in a round, would dance and sing merrily.

Linking the cities, towns and villages were the routes: the roads and ways for travel and passage. Like the network of public Roman roads upon which they had grown, these routes also brought together cultures, races, institutions, people, goods and ideas and thoughts. They were the arteries of the societies of Europe.

***

To reach the Levant, the British gentleman usually sailed from Venice, as pilgrims had done for centuries when on their way to the port of Jaffa and the Holy Land:

> Buy a chest to place your belongings in under seal. In this way you will be able to protect the things which belong to you, like bread, cheese, spices, fruit and other essentials, biscuit for six months, pork, cheese, eggs and fruit to make meals after noon and in the evening, because what you get from the "patron" will be insufficient and you will often be very hungry, and a small chamber pot, because if you become ill and are unable to climb up to the upper parts of the galley you will be able to do what you have to in it.
>
> *- William Wey, Venice, 1462.*

Unlike them, however, he travelled in comfort:

> For seven gold crowns by the month paid by each of us, [the captain] did courteously admit us to his table, and gave us good diet, serving each man with his knife and spoon, and his fork (to hold the meat whiles he cuts it, for they hold it ill manners that one should touch the meat with his hand), and with a glass or cup to drink.
>
> *- Fynes Moryson and his brother on the Little Lion*
> *"at the end of March", 1595.*

The Morysons reached the port of Jaffa on 30 May. Bending down to kiss the land, as was the custom, Henry slipped and fell and smashed his nose, and the accident was seen as a "superstitious sign of ill". On 4 July, near Antakya, southeast Turkey, ill from the flux (dysentery), he died.

Sometimes, instead of sailing all the way from Venice, the British gentleman disembarked at Ragusa (Dubrovnik) and from there crossed the Balkan Peninsula. Later, at the beginning of the seventeenth century, the East Adriatic port city of Split, which was completely rebuilt by Venice for commercial purposes, also became linked to Constantinople by land. It was "the way led by the Jews, who were patrons of the caravans and had businesses in the many cities and towns on the Balkans", explains Sir Henry Blount who made his journey into the Levant from Split in 1634.

Instead of going to Venice, the British gentleman might also have reached the Levant from Hamburg, Germany, by travelling southwards, overland across Eastern Europe through Poland, Ukraine, Moldavia, Romania and Bulgaria. And, of course, he could have sailed directly from England, as Peter Mundy did when he left for Constantinople in 1617:

> In our passage we made calls at Gibraltar, Malaga, Alicante, Majorca, Minorca, Messina in Sicily, Zante, Scandarone or Alexandretta and Chios near Smyrna. At almost all these places were English merchants by whom we were joyfully received and welcomed, our passage being very prosperous and full of various novelties and delights. The only scare was at Cape St. Vincent where the King of Spain's ships met with us at night. Each suspected the other of being Turkish pirates as there were reports of 26 sail being in the vicinity. But, God be praised, we parted friends.

***

To reach Venice from London, the British gentleman followed two routes: a French route and a German route. The French route linked Paris with Lyon and passed over Mont Cenis into Italy.

It had been established during the Champagne trading fairs of the Middle Ages, held in the towns of the Champagne and Brie regions. These fairs had served as the premier market for textiles, leather, fur and spices.

On "the 8th day of April, the 21st year of the reign of our sovereign lord king Henry VII, the year of our Lord God 1506, about 10 o'clock the same night", Sir Richard Guylforde, Lady Guylforde, their chaplain and several servants left Rye in Sussex, England, for the Holy Land. By the next day, they were in Criel-sur-Mer, Normandy, France. They rode to Dieppe and headed south. They passed through Paris, Briere, La Motte, Lyon, Chambery and they crossed the Cottian Alps at Mount Cenis and entered northern Italy. They travelled on to Ambrose, Moncalieri and Alessandria, where they left their horses and "took the water of the Tanaro" for the River Po. Travelling by barge, they passed Pavia, Cremona and Ferrara, and on 16 May, they were in Venice. They spent the rest of the month and the whole of June resting and sightseeing.

The Guylfordes left Venice for the port of Jaffa on 4 July. They sailed towards Istria and passed the gulf of Senj, a place under Hungarian rule where Richard the Lionheart had been shipwrecked on his return home from the Holy Land in 1192. By 6 July, the city of Zadar was sighted, and Lady Guylforde went ashore to attend mass.

During the rest of their voyage, the Guylfordes made stops at the Island of Hvar, Ragusa, Corfu, Morea, Crete, Rhodes and Cyprus, where they met a ship full of pilgrims returning to Venice. They reached Jaffa on 18 August and Sir Richard fell sick. He died on 6 September and was buried on Mount Zion.

Lady Guylforde began her return voyage to Venice on 19 September. On 9 March 1507, "delivered safe from perils and dangers, from the infidels and enemies of Christian faith", she was in England. Her pilgrimage to the Holy Land and back had lasted almost a year.

The alternative German route to Venice linked the cities of Hamburg, Nuremberg, Erfurt, Augsburg and Innsbruck and passed over the Brenner Pass (between Austria and Italy). For centuries, this route had been used by the merchants from the many cities of the Hanseatic League to take their wool, iron and fur products to Venice, to be exchanged for commodities from the East. So important were these merchants to Venice that in 1228 the city built the palace Fondaco dei Tedeschi (see Fig. 11, the building on the left) to serve as a warehouse, business premises and sleeping quarters for them.

On 27 March 1589, accompanied by a merchant friend, a Mr Richard Mallory of London and three servants, one whose name was Fox and who kept the travelogue *His Journey to and from Constantinople*, Harrie Cavendish left the port of Leigh, England for the port of Stade, Hamburg, Germany. For centuries, this regular shipping lane had been used by the Right Worshipful Company of Merchant Adventurers of England to provide the wool that would be spun into yarn and woven into Hamburg's cloth.

From Hamburg, the group travelled south. They passed through many cities and towns, each with a story to tell:

At this town of Erfurt, we were showed an old cloister which in old time maintained fifty monks, but now there be but ten. In this cloister there is an old chapel in which we were showed a tomb of one man lying by two women which was the tomb of an earl of that land who being taken prisoner by the Saracens after long imprisonment obtained the love of a lady of that land by whose mean he obtained liberty and returned into Germany bringing his heathen wife with him, where his German lady received them both lovingly and so was allowed by the bishop of Menz [Mainz] to enjoy them both. His German wife was black and hard favoured but bore him many children; his heathen wife was fair but bore no children. Thus, living till death were buried in this chapel where the memorial of them continues to this day.

At this Shefeld [Seefeld] we were shown a great wonder if it be true. A nobleman of that country refusing to take the blessed sacrament according to the use of the church would take it by himself and in taking it sunk presently down and finding his life going caught hold of the altar stone and gripped it so hard that the print of his hand and fingers remained upon the alter stone to this day. At his sudden death there descended blood from heaven upon him which is kept there still, to the great benefit of the country for that many sick persons have been cured thereby, as they say.

And German hospitality was surely the best in Europe:

> As soon as we had taken up our lodging [in Augsburg], a servant of the house came to us with ink and paper to take our names and of what nation, the which were presently carried to the magistrates of the city. This done we called for supper and fell to it with good stomachs, and being about the midst of our supper there entered into the chamber seven men whereof six of them had the livery of the city which was a long garment half black and half red, and the man that came foremost and single by himself seemed to be a man of more credit than the other six were for they marched by two and two together. The single man had a great pot of wine in his hand and the other six in ether hand a pot, so these seven pots being set down upon the ground in the midst of the room you may suppose that they made a fair show for every pot was full half a yard high and full of good wine. This was a present sent from the lords of the city, the which my master received thankfully and we drank the wine merrily, but the grave man was not so drunk but that he could take my master by that hand which had two dollars in it.

They crossed the Alps at Brenner (Innsbruck, Tyrol), and by 3 May they were in Venice. For three sequins a man, on a frigate of Cattaro (Kotor), Harrie Cavendish found passage to Ragusa.

In Ragusa they slept in the house of a Mr William Robinson, a British gentleman "of many words but slow in performing, for time has so altered the man". And there they saw a "fair church built by an English King" (according to legend, that king was Richard the Lionheart).

For their overland journey across the Balkans to Constantinople, Harrie Cavendish bought a kettle, spices, bread, butter, rice and wine, all carried in a "great bag made of dear's skin dressed with the hair inward". On the "Whitsun Monday", with three Ragusan merchants and a janissary who was their guide, they left:

> Being past Ragusa, which stands in Dalmatia, we came through Serbia and Bosnia and Bulgaria and many other countries. This Serbia and Bosnia be very hilly countries in the which we had not two miles of good way in a day. The people in those countries be very poor as simple in manners as bare in apparel. Their apparel is a white jacket made of very coarse wool, and they make their shoes themselves of a piece of leather tand, and the hair upon it, which they lace to their feet very unhandsomely, and he that can get a red cap of the Greek fashion thinks himself a brave man. In these countries there be no carts nor wagons except some little carts about a poor house. They plough with oxen.

> In these countries the people will call one to another and deliver their minds three miles of one from the other for the hills be so high and the valleys so deep that it will be their half days work to go to their neighbours dwelling. They have great ugly beasts the which they draw wagons with; they call them a buffalo. Two of them will draw as three of their oxen. They use camels for pack horses, which carry a far greater burden than a horse is able to bear. They have no beds in their houses but lie upon boards and benches wrapped in a course rug and upon the ground.

On 16 June, twenty-nine days from Ragusa, they arrived in Constantinople. They spent almost two weeks in the city.

For their return journey to Germany, Harrie Cavendish chose not to travel via Venice, but northwards through Eastern Europe, a route used by the early Crusades. When nearing Yassi, the capital of Moldavia (today's Iasi of Romania), for the first time since their departure from Constantinople they heard the chime of church bells, such was the enormous expanse of the Ottoman Empire. They reached Hamburg on 13 September 1589. Their journey into the Levant and back had been a carefully planned dash.

***

During much of the sixteenth century, the British gentleman followed the German route to Venice. Henry VIII's constant conflicts with France, and Elizabeth I's wars with Spain, were two good reasons for him to do so. From 1562 to 1598 there were, as well, eight Wars of Religion in France between the Catholics and the Protestants. And in the south of Europe was the Inquisition, which attacked all forms of Protestantism after the Reformation. However, when in 1604 Elizabeth I's successor James I made a treaty with Spain, again the British gentleman began to use the French route. "I began my journey through France, hard upon the time when that execrable murder was committed upon the person of Henry IV, by an obscure varlet even in the streets of his principle city, by day, and then when royally attended", wrote George Sandys, who in 1610 made his journey into the Levant.

WILLIAM WEY (1407-1476) was a priest from Devon. For centuries, his travelogue *Matters of Jerusalem* travelled from library to library as a manuscript. In 1857, it was translated into English and published as *The Itineraries of William Wey, Fellow of Eton College: To Jerusalem, A.D. 1458 and A.D. 1462, and to Saint James of Compostella, A.D. 1456* for the Roxburghe Club, the oldest society of bibliophiles in the world. Today, *Matters of Jerusalem* is kept in the Bodleian Library in Oxford. Francis Davey, editor and translator of the 2010 edition of *The Itineraries*, suggests that William Wey may have set off on his final pilgrimage in 1462 as an agent to raise money for either the new king Edward IV, or perhaps for the deposed king Henry VI and Queen Margaret. This was the time of the Wars of the Roses, when the Yorkists who supported Edward IV, and the Lancastrians who supported Henry VI, opposed each other and fought for the throne of England.

SIR RICHARD GUYLFORDE (1455-1506) was a committed follower of the Earl of Richmond (Henry VII and founder of the Tudor dynasty) and probably fought with him at the battle of Bosworth (1485) against Richard III. Sir Richard possessed many skills, especially in the control of artillery and fortifications, engineering and shipbuilding. In 1500, he was elected a Knight of the Garter. By his first wife, Anne Kent, he had two sons and four daughters, and by his second wife, Joan Vaux, one son. His travelogue was probably kept by his chaplain.

HARRIE CAVENDISH (1550-1616) was the eldest son of Sir William Cavendish and his third wife, Elizabeth Hardwick, the celebrated "Bess of Hardwick". One of the wealthiest and most powerful women of the Elizabethan era, she built Hardwick Hall, famous for its "all glass no wall". Harrie Cavendish's godmother was the Lady Elizabeth, later to become Queen of England. In 1568, Harrie married his stepsister, Lady Grace Talbot, and lived with her for most of his life at a Benedictine priory in Tutbury, Staffordshire.

Harrie Cavendish had an explosive personality. He was short tempered and quarrelled with almost everybody and on several occasions was even involved in brawls. He kept minstrels, loved horses and he made visits to London for certain personal reasons.

VENICE

In 1609, wishing "to seclude himself from his soil", William Lithgow visited Venice:

> The city is seven miles in compass, and from so base an abject beginning, it is grown (as it were) to be the chief bulwark of Europe. The laws of this city permit not the younger sons of the best gentry to marry, lest the number increasing should diminish the dignity. Yet nevertheless they permit them unlawful pleasures. The Jews here, and in Rome, wear red, and yellow hats for notice sake to distinguish them from others. And finally, to discourse upon their magnificent arsenal, artillery, munition and armour, the division of streets with channels, the innumerable bridges of stone and timber, their accustomed kind of living, apparel, curtesy and conventions; and the glory of gallants, galleries, galleys, galleasses [ships of war] were a thing for me impossible for me briefly to relate. Wherefore, I desist, concluding thus; this incomparable mansion is the paragon of all the cities in the world.

Always, whenever dissatisfied with England, the British gentleman turned to this famous city, which offered an alternative political view. Had not Sir Thomas Moore, lawyer, writer and saint, based his *Utopia* (1509), a story of a perfect society on an imaginary island, on Venice? In his *Historie of Italie* (1549), William Thomas, a scholar of Italian language and Italian history, explicitly suggested that England should emulate "the city [which] is secure and financially successful". And in his *The Commonwealth of Oceana* (1656), politician, essayist and traveller James Harrington wrote:

Venice is the only commonwealth in the make whereof no man can find a cause of dissolution; for which reason we behold her (though she consists of men that are not without sin) as this day with 1,000 years upon her back, yet for and internal cause, as young, as fresh, and free from decay, or any appearance of it, as she was born.

He had visited the city in 1636, and there, to his delight, was a state unconquered and unaffected by the wars of Europe.

Fig. 5. The Triumphal Quadriga. Author: Tteske. Source: Wikipedia CC. The horses were taken from Constantinople during the infamous sack of the city in 1204. "The Venetians took off the bridles to show that Venice had never been conquered." – Fynes Moryson, 1594.

Fig. 6. Canaletto's *Palazzo Vendramin-Calergi,* a typical *Ca* (an

abbreviation for *Casa*, house), of the Venetian merchants. Source: Wikipedia PD, collection Lord and Lady Wantage. "This was most richly furnished with beds, hangings, tables all rich and curious, the chimney pieces of fine marble, being statues of gods and goddesses. Also a curious garden full of fine devices and marble images. The rent for two months was £20 and to Jews for hire of furniture and plate another £40." – Peter Mundy, 1620.

And although in the Early Modern Age, as the once massive trade of the Mediterranean moved to the Atlantic Ocean, Venice was no longer the entrepôt of Europe, it was still a vibrant cultural and industrial hub with "very many fair shows of wares".

Fig. 7. Canaletto's *Market on the Molo*. Source: Harvard Art Museums/ Fogg Museum, Friends of the Fogg Art Museum Fund, M6480. "This city abounded with good fish, which are twice each day to be sold in two markets of Saint Mark and Rialto, and that it spends weekly 500 oxen and 250 calves, besides great numbers of young goats, hens and many kinds of birds. Victuals were shopped by men, not servants or women, while little boys with baskets carried the goods to the buyer's home." – Fynes Moryson, 1594.

Venice had pioneered the development of foreign exchange,

credit markets, banking and accountancy. In Venice, the payment of debt was guaranteed, else "a pound of flesh".

Venice was the European centre for the production of glass and glassware, including goblets, pitchers, bottles, vases, mirrors, jewellery, candelabra and even spectacles. And in Venice were goldsmiths, mosaicists and woodcarvers.

Venice was where Leonardo da Vinci, Raphael, Michelangelo and Titian, the master of colour, bought the pigments and oil paint upon which their works so much depended. And in Venice were the famous printer-publishers-bookshops Giolito, Giunti and Manuzio. Located in the central districts of San Marco, Sant' Angelo, the Rialto bridge, Santi Apostoli, San Zanipolo and Santa Maria Formosa, they were as well venues where the wealthy met.

Venice was, too, a city of fashion. It produced silk, satin and velvet cloth of the highest quality. Chopines (tall standing shoes) especially were recommended by the Church as they limited a woman's freedom of movement and prevented her from straying and taking pleasure in morally dubious activities, such as dancing.

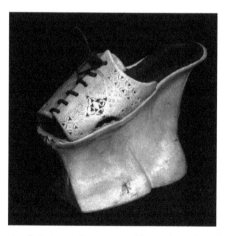

Fig. 8. A reconstructed sixteenth century Venetian chopine. Author: Rama and the Shoe Museum in Lausanne. Source: Wiki CC. "Very near half a yard high from the ground, made of silk, velvet, or leather and richly decorated with precious metals and gems". – Laurence Aldersey, 1581.

By the seventeenth century, Venice had become the most visited tourist centre in Europe, and it all excitedly began in St Mark's Square.

Fig. 9. Canaletto's *St Mark's Square* (c. 1730-1734). Source: Harvard Art Museums/Fogg Museum, Bequest of Grenville L. Winthrop, 1943.106. "The market place of St Mark is paved with bricks, and consists of four market places, joined in one, whereof two may be called the market places of the Duke's Palace. In this market place are solemn spectacles or shows, and all processions made. There they used to muster soldiers, and there the gentlemen and strangers daily meet and walk." — Fynes Moryson, 1594.

Overlooking the square were St Mark's Basilica and the Doge's Palace. In St Mark's were held the religious ceremonies that publicly declared Venice's loyalty to Christianity. In the palace were passed the decisions that shaped much of the Mediterranean world. And so the sacral and the secular were joined together in a triumph of social power. Nearby, too, were the library and the mint. The library housed the rare books brought from Constantinople and Greece and stood for Venice's humanist commitment. The mint, built in a classical Doric-Ionic style, stood for the city's affluence. Not so far away was the Grand Canal and the Rialto bridge – the eighth wonder of the world.

Fig. 10. Canaletto's *Molo with the Library* (1740). Source: Harvard Art Museums/Fogg Museum, Friends of the Fogg Art Museum Fund, M6478. "The inner chamber is called the study, in which many statues, twelve heads of emperors, and other things esteemed precious by all antiquarians. Behind the library is the Mint house (vulgarly called La zecca, whereupon I think the gold coin of the Venetians is called Zecchino) in which house is remarkable that there is no wood in any part thereof, but for fear of fire." – Fynes Moryson, 1594.

Fig. 11. Canaletto's *The Grand Canal with the Rialto Bridge and the Fondaco dei Tedeschi* (1707-1750). Source: Rijksmuseum, Amsterdam, J.W.E. vom Rath Bequest. "It is built of the stone of Istria, upon one arch over the great channel, and the ascent to the top are thirty-six stairs on each side, and upon each side of these stairs are twelve little shops covered with lead: not to speak of the carved images of the blessed Virgin, the Angel Gabriel, and the two protecting saints of the city, namely St Mark, and St Theodore". – Fynes Moryson, 1594.

By then, as well, Venice was at the heart of the British gentleman's Grand Tour. In 1637, the city opened the world's first opera house. The fascinating paintings of Canaletto (1697-1768), Pietro Longhi (1701-1785) and Francesco Guardi (1712-1793), who immortalised the views of Venice – the canals, the buildings, the squares, the bridges – and chronicled the affairs of everyday Venetian life – the events, the festivities, the processions, the amusements – were very famous. And there were the social comedies of Carlo Goldoni (1707-1793) and Pietro Chiari (1712-1785), which were full of wit and honesty. But perhaps the best entertainments in Venice were the magnificent concerts of the "noble Venetians, called il Philarmonici":

> At eleven we get up and breakfast: at twelve we walk to St. Mark's Place, where everything that is brilliant assembles. We dine a half after three, and go to bed till seven, when we dress, and are taken in our gondola to the Fresco…Between nine and ten we frequent the coffee-houses – the resort of all fashionable people, even the ladies, who are as numerous there as the gentlemen…At eleven the operas begin, where we pass the time in visits from one box to another until they end, which generally happens about three.
>
> –*Thomas Watkins, 1785.*

What really made Venice so immensely popular, though, was its famous Carnival. It fed the endless imaginations of the visitors to make the city the most licentious tourist destination in Europe.

LAURENCE ALDERSEY (1546-1598) was a sea captain from Cheshire. He made two journeys into the Levant: in 1581 from Venice, and in 1586 directly from Bristol. As was then the practice amongst merchants and ship captains, he "set down by himself" a record of his travels abroad. Like most other British gentlemen of the Early Modern Age, Laurence was a Protestant. During one journey on his way to Jerusalem, "seven leagues past Zante", following a great storm, he was asked by "the [ship's] purser to kiss the image of our Lady". Because he refused to do so, he almost lost his life. "There was a great stir: the patron and all the friars were told of it, and every one said I was a Lutheran", he recalled.

RAGUSA

Well connected to the Balkans, from its very beginnings in the seventh century when it was founded as a refuge from the Slavs, Ragusa (Dubrovnik) was a conduit for trade. From nearby inland Bosnia and Serbia the city imported and resold wax, cattle, leather, wood timber, honey and, in the thirteenth and fourteenth centuries, silver. From an industrialised Italy, it imported woollen cloth and textiles. And Ragusa's lucrative sea salt from Ston (Pelješac Peninsula), or Stagnum – meaning still water, as the Romans called this area – was sold throughout the whole of Europe. Additionally, Ragusa had magnificent argosy ships. Built in the city's shipyards of Santa Croce, Lopud, Šipan, Orebić, Cavtat, Ston and Zaton, these "pageants of the sea" were financed through shares.

Ragusa was an oligarchy: ruled by a few who directed power efficiently. Unlike much of the rest of Europe, it was never subjected to the control of a monarchy or ruled by one.

Ragusa's bureaucrats were appointed on merit. They were not hereditary aristocrats, and competition was advocated in all aspects of life. "Only free trade and a free money market can provide the capital needed for commercial enterprises and create the wealth of peoples and individuals", wrote the Ragusan economist Benedikt Kotruljević in his *Book on the Art of Trade* published in 1475.

Ragusa minted its own money: the copper folar and the silver thaler, denar and perpera. It had a pharmacy that provided free medical care to all Ragusans, free schools, a public water supply with many fountains and a sewage system. And Ragusa's lazaretto, or a house of quarantine, was the first to be built on the Adriatic.

In 1526, faced with a Venetian threat, Ragusa voluntarily put itself under the protection of the Ottoman sultan. It was a brilliant diplomatic move. For the next hundred years, all Ottoman trade on the Adriatic went through the city. With an incredible income of

Fig. 12. The massive, seemingly endless fortress walls of Ragusa. Source: Dubrovnik State Archives. An old aquarelle. Author unknown. "It is the strongest town of walls, towers, bulwarks, watches and wards that ever I saw in all my life."
– Sir Richard Guylforde's chaplain, 1506.

over a million ducats a year, Ragusa had financially surpassed even Venice.

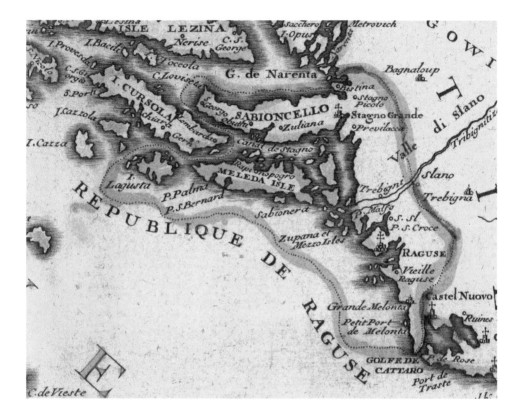

Fig. 13. Map of the Republic of Ragusa (1716). Author: Nicolas de Fer. Source: David Rumsey Historical Map Collection. "Ragusa is a commonwealth governed by senators, and a senate council; it is wonderful strong, and also well-guarded (with massive walls), being situated by the sea side, it has a fine haven and many goodly ships: The greatest traffic they have with the Genoans. Their territory in the firm land is not much in respect of the neighbouring Turks, but they have certain commodious islands, which to them are profitable: And notwithstanding of the great strength and riches they possess, yet for their better safeguard and liberty, they pay a yearly tributary pension unto the great Turk, amounting to fourteen-thousand sequins of gold: yea, and also they pay yearly a tributary pension onto the Venetians, for the islands reserved by them in the Adriatic Gulf, so that by both sea and land they are made tributary citizens. The most part of the civil magistrates, have but the half of their heads bare, but the vulgar sort are all shaven like to the Turks." – William Lithgow, 1609.

But nature was soon to strike Ragusa a deadly blow. On Wednesday, 6 April 1667, the city was hit by a "terrible and fatal earthquake". The English newspaper, the *Savoy*, wrote about it:

About three or four in the afternoon, there happened a terrible and fatal earthquake, which in a moment threw down and ruined the palace, that was the usual place of residency of their Duke, but now his tomb, himself with his attendants being buried together in its ruins. The same fate also ran all the palaces, churches, monasteries and houses of that city, all of them by the violence of the earthquake turned upside down, with as great a destruction to the inhabitants; which was much increased by the tumbling down of great stones from the neighbouring mountains: which falling likewise upon the destroyed city, made of it all one great confused heap of ruins.

There happened at the same instant a great wind, which occasioned one mischief to fall upon the neck of another; for this meeting with some fire, which lay mixed with the combustible matter that fell on it confusedly in the ruins, caused a great and violent flame; which continued many days, to the infinite infliction of the poor survivors of that dreadful calamity; who were but few in number, not exceeding 600 persons, and about 25 of their nobility. It was a lamentable spectacle to behold the greater part of this small remainder, pitifully wounded and maimed crawling as astonished persons through the ruined streets, with their beads about their necks, begging for mercy and pardon for their sins, every minute expecting death.

The castle, which was very strong, was twice observed to open and then close again, and the sea to retire at least four times: all the fountains about the city are also dried up, so that there remains not any water to make them drink: only the fort, made up of earth, continues whole.

That upon the sea, with the doana or custom-house, and the hospital, received some damage, but it is believed may in some little space of time be repaired. Several voices have been heard under the ruins, where persons lay buried alive, many of which, have by the compassion of those that escaped, with much pains in removing the wood and stones that covered them, been brought out alive, after four or five days continuance in that miserable condition; confessing, That they were only kept alive by drinking their own urine.

Ragusa's painstaking recovery lasted a century. In 1778, Thomas Watkins visited the city:

But, this evil [the earthquake], as it often happens, was productive of good; for to it must be ascribed the breadth and regularity of its streets, the grandeur of the public buildings, and the beauty of the houses.

Fig. 14. Villa Sorkočević at Lapad, Dubrovnik (1521). Source: Villas Croatia. "Into it [the sea] flows the broad river Ambla, from its deep and silent recesses of rocks and mountains covered with olive groves, and enlivened with villas – the summer residence of the noble Ragusans." – Thomas Watkins, 1778.

Complementing the summer residences were the beautiful gardens. Filled with orange and lemon trees, myrtle, laurel, cypress, jasmine, oleander, carnations and violets, and shaped by meandering paths covered with pergolas of sweet wine, stone walls, steps, terraces and belvederes, benches, seats, fountains and ponds, the gardens served the Renaissance ideal of linking man with nature.

As was obligatory in those days, Thomas Watkins had first to do quarantine:

> On my arrival I was permitted by the superior of the health office to perform my quarantine on shore (instead of on the islands of Mrkan and Bobara, in the vicinity of Cavtat), and hired a house for the purpose; but through the interposition of the Senator Count Basegli (to whom I brought a letter of introduction from Mr. Paul their Consul at Patras) instead of being confined forty days, I was liberated in three weeks, although we had arrived with a foul bill of health: – an indulgence without precedent. Indeed when in quarantine I had the liberty of walking or riding wherever I pleased with an attendant, though at first, for form sake, a sentinel was placed at my door. They insisted (for I was scrupulous) that I, and even my servant go out, being persuaded we would not touch anybody.

By chance, his release coincided with "the grand festival of Biagio [St Blaise]", the city's patron saint, and he was "honoured with a seat among the nobles to behold the ancient ceremonies of the Republic":

> The principal of these were a religious procession, and rustic dance of old women, who carried upon their heads baskets of bread to denote plenty. Upon this day, a numerous body of peasantry assembles in the city, every man bearing his musket, which he continually loads and discharges, being supplied by Government with an unlimited quantity of powder.

Thomas Watkins remained in Ragusa for several weeks:

> Of the Ragusans I cannot write too favourably, especially of the nobles and superior order of citizens, who (generally speaking) possess all the good qualities that virtuous example and refined education can bestow, without those vices which prevail in countries more open to foreign intercourse, and

consequently more practiced in deception. They have more learning and less ostentation than any people I know, more politeness to each other, and less envy. Their hospitality to strangers cannot possibly be exceeded: in short, their general character has in it so few defects, that I do not hesitate to pronounce them (as far as my experience of other people will permit me) *the wisest, best and happiest of states.*

In her *Renaissance Man*, published in 1967, the famous Hungarian philosopher Agnes Heller wrote that if freedom is the starting point and goal of the human essence, the means of achieving that goal are intellect and work which (combined with freedom) give creativity, self-creation, versatility, dissatisfaction and limitlessness with respect to knowledge. This was Ragusa, "the wisest, best and happiest of states." It was a city of playwrights, painters and sculptors, composers, philosophers, mathematicians and beautiful women.

Fig. 15. A portrait of Cvijeta (Flora) Zuzorić (year unknown). Author unknown. Source: Dubrovnik State Archives. The most celebrated and most beautiful Ragusan woman of her time, Cvijeta became an object of envy, and in 1583, moved to Ancona, Italy, where she lived for the rest of her life. So enchanted was the poet Giulio Mosti with her that he asked his friend, the great poet Torquato Tasso, to write about her. Tasso dedicated three sonnets and five madrigals to "a Ragusan lady who lives in Ancona".

THOMAS WATKINS (eighteenth century) was a clergyman from Brecknock, South Wales. His *Travels through Switzerland, Italy, Sicily, the Greek Islands to Constantinople, through part of Greece, Ragusa, and the Dalmatian Isles*, consists of the thirty-six letters he wrote to his father. In one, dated 15 June 1788, sent from Venice, he recalls a story he was told when previously visiting Geneva:

> A foreign gentleman happened to sit down in a coffee-house near a person who declaimed violently against the state inquisitors, or three principal magistrates. The discourse was addressed to this stranger, who not only declined saying anything upon the subject, but withheld (as far as was consistent with civility) his attention with the speaker. The next night, on coming to his lodgings, he was seized, blindfolded, and forced into a gondola, threatened with instant death if he spoke, and carried off in profound silence. On landing, he was led but a little way before he entered a house; where, on the bandage being taken off his eyes, he found himself in a large apartment hung with black, before a tribunal as terrible in appearance as the inquisition. Those who sat as judges, asked him how long he had known his companion in the coffee-house: he protested he had never seen him before, and gave such convincing proofs of his innocence, that after a short consultation, they ordered him to be enlarged, enjoining him, however, not only to be silent upon political subjects as long as he remained in Venice, but even to listen to them in future. He was then led through a long passage into a chamber as dismal as the former, at the upper end of which he saw a man hanging by the throat upon a hook; on coming nearer to the body – he perceived it with horror to be the person he had seen in the coffee-house.

Thomas Watkins' letters are a good example of the fine art of worldly conduct expected from the British gentleman of that time.

CONSTANTINOPLE

Constantinople was born in 330 on the Strait of Bosporus near a Greek settlement called Byzantium. It was to be the new Roman capital for a new Eastern Roman Empire. The whole world was stripped bare to build it, so it was said.

By sea, Constantinople was reached through Hellespont Strait and the wide and deep estuary of the Golden Horn. By land, it was linked to the Western Roman colonies of the East Adriatic by the long road Via Egnatia.

In the fifth century, the Emperor Theodosius built the city's awesome walls that embraced 1800 hectares. Impregnable, they would withstand the attacks of the Slavs, Arabs, Persians, Bulgarians and the Rus (ancestors of today's Russians).

By the twelfth century, Constantinople was an international commercial centre connected to Europe, Egypt, Russia, China and India, and it possessed two thirds of all the wealth of the known world. It was a home of learning, Greek culture and an unparalleled art form known as Byzantine art. It contained the largest church in Christendom – Hagia Sophia. And, according to historical sources, in Constantinople were the English halberdiers who clashed their weapons together to make a terrible sound and wished the Emperor a long life in the English tongue.

In 1204, Constantinople was sacked by the Crusaders and made a part of the Latin Empire until 1261 when it was freed by Michael Palaeologus, a general from Nicaea. Once more, in 1453, Constantinople was conquered, this time by the Turks. They renamed the city Istanbul.

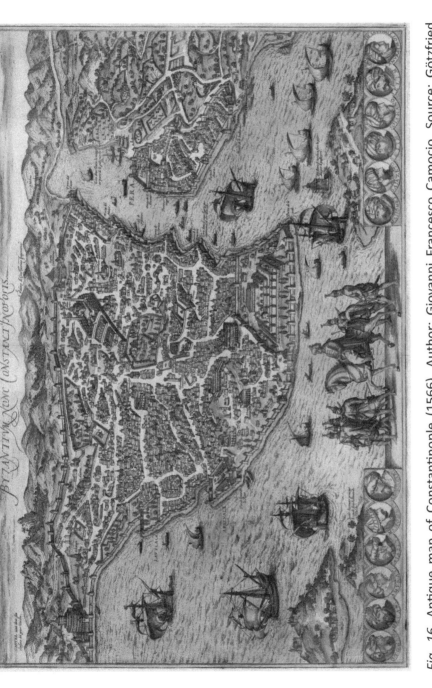

Fig. 16. Antique map of Constantinople (1566). Author: Giovanni Francesco Camocio. Source: Götzfried Antique Maps. "It stands on a cape of land near the entrance of the Bosporus. In form triangular: on the East-side washed with the same, and on the North-side with the haven, adjoining on the west to the Continent. Walled with brick and stone, intermixed orderly: having four and twenty gates and posterns; whereof five do regard the land and nineteen the water; being thirteen miles in circumference." – George Sandys, 1604.

Fig. 17. Panorama of Constantinople with the Fatih Mosque (1559). Author: Melchior Lorck. Source: Wikipedia PD. "The 9. of September we arrived at the great and most stately City of Constantinople, which for the situation and proud seat thereof, for the beautiful and commodious havens, and for the great and sumptuous buildings of their Temples, which they call Moschea, is to be preferred before all the Cities of Europe." – Master Henry Austell, 1585.

Fig. 18. Tersane Garden, Istanbul (1453). Authors: Nurhan Atasoy and Seyit Ali Kahraman. Source: Istanbul University Central Library. "And there the Emperor of the Turks then living, whose name was Amurat, kept his Court and residence, in a marvellous goodly place, with divers gardens and houses of pleasure, which is at the least two English miles in compass, and the three parts thereof joins upon the sea." – Master Henry Austell 1585.

The gardens stood for eternal life, filled with spiritual and physical happiness. They symbolised paradise as described in the Quran, "with streams of water that will not go rank, and rivers of milk whose taste will not undergo a change, and rivers of wine delectable to drinkers, and streams of purified honey, and fruits of every kind in them, and forgiveness from their lord". Paradise was very important to the Ottomans and they symbolised it in all of their architecture and spaces of everyday life. Trees, especially the cypress tree, and water were a natural way to do this.

Not a Catholic city, Constantinople was never a moral threat for the Protestant British gentleman. As Hubert Languet, Sir Philip Sidney's mentor, explained: "unlike as in Rome, a Protestant in Constantinople did not incur a hazard of losing one's religion, one's conscience, one's reputation". On the other hand, Sir Philip never visited Constantinople, because the journey was far too risky for a man of his social rank. The plague, for example, was constantly present in Constantinople:

It is exceeding great in that city, and after such an odious manner that those who are infected (before they die) have the half of their one side rot, and fall away, so that you may easily discern the whole entrails of their bowls. – *William Lithgow, 1609.*

Nevertheless, Constantinople was the best place for the young British gentlemen of the Early Modern Age to learn about the Turks' religion and customs, what Sir Philip Sidney called "mores":

… knowledge of the which stand in the things which are in themselves either simply good or simply evil, and so serve for a right instruction, or a shunning example.

Fig. 19. The Slave Market (1838). Author: William Allan. Source: Scottish National Gallery. "I have seen men and women as usually sold here in markets, as horses and other beasts are with us. The most part are of which Hungarians, Transylvanians, Carinthians, Istrians, and Dalmatian captives, and of other places besides which they can overcome." – William Lithgow, 1609.

The Turkish mores made, too, for a good story:

> I have seen sometimes two thousand Turks travelling to
> Mecca, in pilgrimage; which is in Arabia Felix: where
> many in a superstitious devotion, having seen the Tomb of
> Mahomet, are never desirous to see the vanities of the world
> again: For in a frantic piety they cause a smith to pull forth
> their eyes: And these men are called afterwards Hoggeis, that
> is, Holy Men, whom the Turks much honour, and regard: and
> are always led about from town to town by men hands, and
> fed, and regarded like unto princes, or like the Capushines
> that scourge themselves on Good Friday, met, and homaged
> at every passing street, with prayers, gifts, and adorations.
>
> *–William Lithgow, 1609.*

But it was always Constantinople of the past, "the old seat of
Christian Emperors", that the British gentleman really admired. He
lamented the Turks' occupation of the city and their domination of
the Greeks who, in the words of George Sandys:

> … once so glorious, and famous for their happy estate are
> now through vice and ingratitude, become the most deplored
> spectacles of extreme misery: the wild beasts of mankind
> having broken in upon them, and rooted out all civilities;
> and the pride of a stern and barbarous tyrant possessing the
> thrones of ancient and just dominion.

Under the Turks, Constantinople had become, to borrow
from the great French historian Fernand Braudel and his *The
Mediterranean*, "an urban monster". Eight galleys of grain a day
were needed to feed its population. Thousands of products were
sold and bought within its walls. Yet it produced nothing: it lived
off an Ottoman Empire that survived only as long as it grew.

In 1809, the famous Lord Byron made his journey into the
Levant. Ten years later the world would read:

The mountains look on Marathon –
And Marathon looks on the sea;
And musing there an hour alone,
I dreamed that Greece might still be free.

Don Juan (1819-24)

On 7 May 1832, in the Treaty of Constantinople, Greece was recognised as an independent nation. Constantinople remained Istanbul.

GEORGE SANDYS (1577-1664) was the youngest son of Edwin Sandys, archbishop of York, and was educated at St Mary Hall, Oxford. In April 1621 he was appointed treasurer of the London Company and sailed to Virginia, America, with the new governor, Sir Francis Wyatt. He remained there some ten years, afterwards returning to England for good. George Sandys's *Relation of a Journey Begun An. Dom. 1610* was reprinted nine times and greatly contributed towards a knowledge of geography and ethnology.

MASTER HENRY AUSTELL came from a merchant family. Little is known about him.

A VOYAGE

On 20 June 1675, "the wind being fair, though so gentle a gale, and the water so smooth", Sir George Wheler and Monsieur Jacob Spon, a "Doctor of Physic" from Lyon, France, who Sir George had met during his previous travels abroad, left Venice aboard the Venetian galley *Il Hercule in Cunea* for Constantinople, from where they wished to travel into Greece. The gentlemen would sail the East Adriatic, which was under Venetian rule, and tramp the Greek islands, which were partly under Venice and partly under the Ottomans. All in all, a safe voyage was anticipated with many stops at the cities and towns and islands.

To prepare himself for his journey, Sir George had read Strabo's *Geographica* and George Sandys's *A Relation*. As an antiquarian and botanist, he especially wished to study the local monuments as well as the plants and herbs of the Mediterranean. In the Early Modern Age, antiquarianism was regarded as the foundation for all historical studies, while botany was an independent scientific discipline founded on identification and classification. The botanic gardens of Padua, Pisa and Florence, for example, had been founded in the middle of the sixteenth century, and in England, the University of Oxford Botanic Garden in 1621.

In 1682, Sir George published his *A Journey into Greece*. He wrote, he tells the reader, as "a Christian, Traveller, and Philosopher", but adds:

> As to the curious plants, I would have added more cuts, most of them which I have described, being either unknown or very rare in our parts; but indeed, the bookseller was very unwilling to be burthened with them, the change of graving being too great for his profit.

For the next hundred years *A Journey into Greece* was to be the definite reference on that part of the world.

THE EAST ADRIATIC

Fig. 20. The Adriatic Sea, which was named so by the Greeks after the Illyrian word *adur*, meaning water. Source: Blue Water Holidays.

Ten thousand years ago, the north of the Adriatic was land and home to Europe's hordes of roaming animals and the hunter-gatherers who followed them. As temperatures rose and the surrounding glaciers melted, the Adriatic Sea formed. Vegetation and forests spread and a way of life centred around a technology of flints emerged.

Agriculture reached Europe from Anatolia around 7000 BC. Instead of caves, people now lived in villages consisting of groups of huts within ditched enclosures. They hunted, fished, gathered plants, began to herd sheep and goats and farmed. Along the better part of the East Adriatic, the Hvar culture (originating from the island of Hvar), dominated. The pottery of these people was finely glazed, coloured and decorated with characteristic "impresso" patterns created through impressions with shells.

In the same way agriculture gave a new way of life, so too did the development of metallurgy. It had originated in the ancient Near East with copper, which by 3000 BC was replaced by bronze. At that time, gold, "the glory of the immortals and a sign of wealth among ordinary humans", was also being used as an ornament. Around 2000 BC, bronze was in Europe, and a thousand years later, iron arrived.

During the first millennium BC, a militarily superior force of Indo-European tribes – the Illyrians, as the Greeks later called these people, settled along the East Adriatic. To the north were the Histri and Liburni, while to the south were the Delmati, Daorsi and the Ardiaei. The Illyrians lived in stone huts within fortified enclosures of dry stone walls built on naturally protected sites.

Five hundred years later, the Greeks were also on the East Adriatic, as a part of their massive colonisation of the Mediterranean. They established the city of Durres (Albania); colonies on the islands of Vis, Hvar and Korčula; and the two trading centres of Trogir and Stobreč near Split. With them, they brought the olive tree and the vine, and they introduced the systematic cultivation of the land. But their presence did not last. By 230 BC, it was all but wiped out by the Illyrians. A brief golden moment of Greek civilisation on the East Adriatic was brought to an end.

By the beginning of the first century BC, after three wars with Carthage, the Romans had conquered the whole of the Mediterranean. They called it *Mare Nostrum*, Our Sea. Excluding Venice and Istria, which formed Regio X, the Tenth Region of the Roman Empire, the East Adriatic was named Dalmatia (meaning a land of shepherds), and Dalmatia together with the Roman province of Pannonia (a region today divided between Croatia, Hungary and Serbia) was referred to as Illyricum.

Along the East Adriatic, colonies of Roman citizens and army veterans were planted, and the city of Salona, near Split, was made the capital of Dalmatia. Indeed, those were prosperous times. Roads, viaducts, fortifications, palaces, amphitheatres, spas and churches were built and whole regions were engaged in the production of olive oil and the manufacture of amphorae. The Pax Romana had made the Mediterranean a peaceful Roman lake.

As with the rest of the Roman world, at the end of the fifth century, Illyricum was invaded by the Germanic and Slavic tribes. Such were their numbers that not even the grass would grow where they had marched, so it was said. And – although later, much of Illyricum, along with the rest of the western Mediterranean coast of Italy, Spain and Africa, was re-conquered by the intact Byzantine, or Eastern Roman Empire – again the barbarians returned. Seeking safety, the people of the East Adriatic fled to the fortified coastal cities and islands.

By the seventh century, the East Adriatic was the home of the descendants of Roman settlers and Latinised Illyrians whose towns were nominally under Byzantine rule, while in the rural hinterland, Pannonia, were the Slavs. Eventually, Christianity, trade and the need to centralise resources would bring these people together.

Meanwhile, in Pannonia, the Croats, a people who arrived with the Slavs, had founded their Kingdom of Croatia. They were a powerful military force with an army of "sixty thousand horse and one hundred thousand foot". For defeating Bulgarian forces in the "Battle of the Bosnian Highlands" in 926, the Byzantine Emperor Constantine awarded the Croatian King Tomislav jurisdiction over the East Adriatic cities of Zadar, Trogir and Split, and the northern East Adriatic islands of Krk, Cres, Lošinj, Rab, Ugljan and Pašman. Split was chosen to be the centre of the Croatian Church.

Yet the Kingdom of Croatia did not last. On 20 April 1089, in Knin, a town near Split, during a rally to raise an army to help the Pope free Jerusalem from the Turks, the king of Croatia, Zvonimir, was murdered by his own people, who were opposed to the war. "May you never have a king of your own blood", he cried out as they charged forward and slashed at his body. So it was written in the (alleged) medieval Chronicle of the Priest of Duklja.

***

Il Hercule in Cunea crossed the Gulf of Venice and headed

towards the northern Istrian town of Rovinj. There, in the summer months, lived the pilots who steered the galleys over the dangerous flats that lay before Venice. Sometimes a vessel "had but half a foot, and sometimes not but an inch of water below its keel", Sir George was told. But first, a stop was made at the nearby islet of St Andrew with its convent of Franciscan friars, where Sir George spent a whole afternoon, "made pleasant by the delightful prospects of the woods, hills, and sea".

Around Rovinj were large olive orchards, vineyards and plantations. They had been developed in the thirteenth century to meet the dramatic rise in demand for food created by the expanding cities and towns under Venice. People always wanted wine and the experience of its happy relationship with life. Believed to be nutritious, it was drunk in large quantities.

Fig. 21. Ottoman map of the coastline from Rovinj north (early sixteenth century). Artist: Piri Reis. Source: Wikipedia PD. "It is not big but seems populous and is a Bishop's see. There are so many decrepit persons there, strong wine being the producer of gouts and sciatica's."

The next day they arrived in Pula. "One of the most ancient cities of Istria, with a spacious port, every way land-locked", it had a fascinating history:

The Poet, Callimachus, affirms it was a colony of Cholcis, who pursued the Argonauts by Sea; whom having lost in the pursuit, and not daring to return to their King, they voluntarily banished themselves, [from] their country, and planted this. Wherefore their city was called Pola; which signifies (if we may believe Strabo) a banished people. Nor can they agree what way they took to come to this place. Some will have it, that they came by the Euxin-Sea, up the Danube, formerly called Ister; which made them give the name of Istria to the country they came to inhabit; and that they afterwards sailed in the Adriatic Sea with the same vessels: a thing impossible, unless they carried them upon their shoulders; the Danube having not communication with the Venetian Gulf.

Following the Roman Civil war of 42 BC, Pula had been completely rebuilt with a water supply and sewage system. However, "the marks of its greatness", Sir George observed, were in its monuments: the Triumphant-arch, the Temple of Augustus and the huge amphitheatre.

Fig. 22. The Town of Pula (c. 1780). Author: Marco Sebastiano Giampiccoli. Source: Archaeological Museum of Istria.

Exploring the surrounding area, Sir George found common sage and winter savoury. They were just two of the many wild plants of the East Adriatic used by people in their everyday lives.

From Pula, *Il Hercule in Cunea* crossed the Kvarner bay and sailed towards the island of Lošinj. This sea was known for its violent storms and, sure enough, they were suddenly met with "such thundering, lightening and rain, as if the elements had conspired to their destruction". Forced to seek shelter, they slept out the night.

In the morning, in a background of blue, the islands of Silba and Olib were sighted, and as if having sailed in a "river between little islands", they entered Dalmatia. It was 25 June.

Fig. 23. Rock samphire. Source: Martina Bogdanić. "The mariners gathered great quantities to boil and eat with oil and vinegar."

As *Il Hercule in Cunea* approached the port of Zadar, a cannon shot was fired from the fort:

It saluted the bailo [*Il Hercule in Cunea*'s captain], as also did the musketeers from the walls; and upon his arrival in the port, the count and captain of the [Venetian] military-forces received him at his landing. They were clothed in crimson suits and gowns, made something like the civilians' gowns at Oxon. The bailo also was in a crimson suit, but made after the French fashion. These, with the militia, conducted him to the palace of the general of Dalmatia, who resides there.

Zadar was the commercial centre of Dalmatia and was strongly fortified. The Venetian military forces in the city "consisted of eight companies of foot, and three of horse, being for the most part Morlachs, Croats, and other people of the mountains and northern parts of Dalmatia".

Fig. 24. Sir George Wheler's sketch of a Morlach: "Their habit is odd. For shoes they have only a piece of leather or sometimes of a dried skin, fitted to, and by thongs or laces going cross-ways over the back of the feet, are tied fast to their feet. Their legs are covered with buskins of cloth, or leather; to which are joined a pair of red breeches, being the colour they much delight in. Their doublet has no sleeves, but are supplied by those of their shirt; which are long and wide, without any

binding at the wrists; but open like a surplice, and edged about with a lace. Their long caps are of red cloth, flapping or hanging down on one side, and adorned with a stone, wherein are set three pieces of iron in form of Feathers. Such was their strength, as four of them could take a man on horse-back upon their shoulders and carry them both over the straights and dangerous places of the mountains, even sometimes twenty, or thirty paces at a time."

Sir George and Monsieur Spon spent almost a week in Zadar, resting and seeing the countryside, which was "well cultivated and planted", although "not a tree had been left to stand since they had some squirmings with the Turks". On the second day of their stay, they visited the governor, a Signior Antonio Soderino, to see his collection of gold coins and medals. Unknown to them, while they were there, he sent for their baggage and insisted that they "made his palace their inn".

Fig. 25. The relics of St Simeon in the Church of St Simeon in Zadar. Source: Croatian Conservation Institute, Zagreb. "It [the body of St Simeon] was brought from the Holy Land; and being worshipped with great devotion, is often carried in procession about the town, as being their patron and protector. It has a glass on one side of its shrine, to expose it to the view of the devout, and yet to keep it from the injury of weather. It appears of a whitish colour, much like to those I have seen at Toulouse in France, at the Church of the Cordeliers; where all the bodies buried there, in the space of one year, become as dry as any mummy".

On 1 July, "the wind being fair, and a brisk gale", *Il Hercule in Cunea* left Zadar for Split. They passed "between the land and several little islands, which make a channel like to a river, deep enough for galleys, but not for ships of any burthen". They saw Old Zadar where the people planted "olives and vines, which bear good muskadel-wines, and in great plenty". And somewhat further on was Murter with "its splendid port". Sir George found many wild plants on this island, including a "plant with leaves, like althea for shape, but of a deep green, and smooth, sending up a stalk above a yard and a half high, full of milk". He thought it was probably "*campanula major lactescens lobelia*".

Il Hercule in Cunea did not stop at Šibenik, "the strongest city of Dalmatia belonging to the State of Venice". Nevertheless, with the help of a "perspective glass", Sir George did see the city's famous cathedral of St. James. It had been built by the master craftsman George of Dalmatia who worked on it until his death in 1475. Inspired by construction methods used in shipbuilding, he had used no mortar or bolts, but instead, fitted the large slabs of stone together in perfect joints.

On 3 July, they were in Split.

Fig. 26. A View of Split (1764). Author: Robert Adam. Source: Wikipedia PD. "The town is situated on the south coast at the bottom of a bay, in the bending shape of a half-moon, which makes a deep haven and a good anchorage, but somewhat open to the south winds. Its situation is very remarkable. The land whereon it stands being a peninsula, joined to the firm land of Dalmatia by an isthmus of about a mile over. It is

walled in by a prodigious precipice of mountains, ranged along those coasts. It has only one entrance into the firm land by a very narrow passage which is defended by a fort [Klis] built upon a rock just in the entrance, about eight miles northward from the city."

During their stay in Split, Sir George and Monsieur Spon slept in the city's lazaretto. It was located in the remains of a huge palace built by the Roman Emperor Diocletian at the turn of the fourth century AD. The food in Split was excellent – and very cheap:

> For they pay not for partridges above a groat, or five-pence apiece; a hare not much more, and butcher's meat not above a penny a pound. Here is plenty of little young tortoises, which they sell very cheap, and esteem good meat. But the trout that are caught in the little river running through Salona are held exquisite, and were famous in the time of the emperor Diocletian; who was so pleased with them, that he made a channel from the river to his palace, there to preserve them. There is plenty of good fruit here; the season then yielded cherries, mulberries, figs, and abundance of apricots; but of the last, I never found any so fair, nor well-tasted as those of England.

The area around the city was "full of vines, olives, corn, pomegranates, and other curious plants". Of the ancient city of Salona, which was once "about seven or eight miles in circuit, although they report it to have been more", only ruins remained. The not-so-faraway fort of Klis, however, was a "very strong fort, and that more by nature than art".

Fig. 27. Liberation of Klis in 1648. Author: Leonardo Foscolo. Source: Museum of the Cetinska Krajina Region. "It stands just in the middle of the passage between the mountains, whose height and precipices

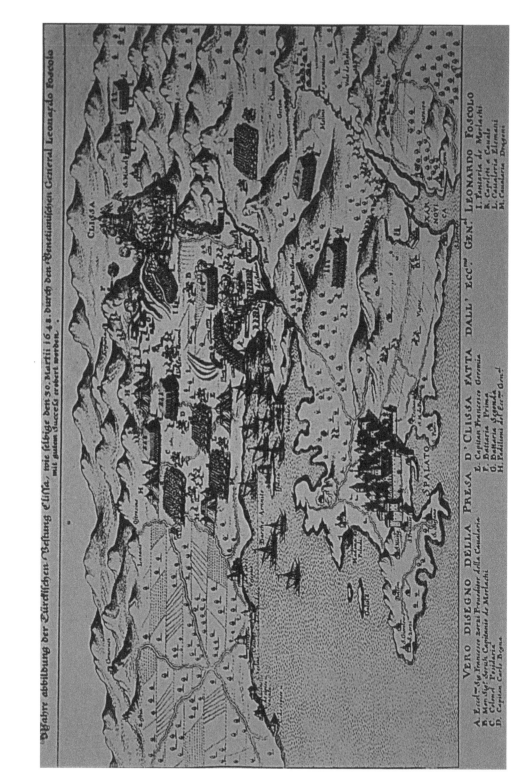

Wahre abbildung der Türckischen Bestung Clissa, wie selbige den 30. Martii 1648 durch den Venetianischen General Leonardo Foscolo mit gutem Success erobert worden.

VERO DISEGNO DELLA PRESA D'CLISSA FATTA DALL' ECC^{mo} GEN^l LEONARDO FOSCOLO

A. Eccel=Sig. Francesco zorzi Provedsior della Cavalleria.
B. Mon.Sig. Serub Capitanio de Mordachi.
C. Colonel Vesilaria
D. Capitan Carli Bigna

E. Capitan Francesco Geremia
F. Battaria Prima
G. Battaria Segonda
H. P. dlituni L'Ecc^{mo} G.nel

I. Tentaria de Mordachi
K. Cavlleria a Cavali
L. Cavalleria Elemani
M. Cavalaria Dragoni

are such, as leave no other entrance into the inland-parts from the peninsulas, but this. And this is so narrow, that not a man or horse can pass by without the licence of the castle. It [the fort] was taken from the Turks by the Venetians and that as much by an accident, as by the vigorous assaults that were made against it. The Turks were frightened into a capitulation, by a granado that fell upon the mosque, whilst they were at their devotions, and did such mischief as quite discouraged them from holding out any longer. They therefore surrendered on condition of free passage with bag and baggage; which although granted by the commander, yet was little use to them. For the Morlachs, their inveterate enemies, way-laid them in their passage, and cut all their throats, without his knowledge. They say that it [Klis] did formerly belong to the Emperor of Germany, and was built by a Queen of Hungary."

At two o'clock on a Sunday morning, 13 July, they set sail for the island of Hvar: "the isle Ptolomy called Pharia, and Strabo Pharos".

It has a good haven at the south-end, where the town is called the name of the Isle. It represents the form of a theatre; whereof the town possess the place of the spectators: yet appears most beautiful to those that enter the area; which is the port; being built in several degrees one above another, according to the rising of the ground; having a citadel on the top of a steep rock, backed with exceeding high mountains. It lies against the south, and hath a harbour, secured from that wind by the rocks, that lie before it. They have beautified the shore on each side with a good mole, made out of the rocks, which there are in too great plenty. To conclude, it has good moorage, and is deep enough for ships at any rate [size].

On Hvar, everybody worked. Ships were built, hundreds of sailors were catered for, and wool and sheep and goat cheese were in great demand. But the "greatest trade" of Hvar was the "fishing of sardelli [pilchards]":

In May and June, they are caught here, and upon the Shore of Dalmatia near Vis, south of this isle, in such abundance, that they furnish all Parts of Italy and Greece with them. The Turks take them as physick [medicine], when they are sick. They follow a light and flock together about a boat that carries it in the night; and so are caught with great facility.

Hvar was also known for its salted fish, most of which was sent to Venice so that its citizens always had "a supply of sufficient food at affordable prices". Wishing to see the sea around him, Sir George climbed the island's highest mountain "where were the watch-men, who gave notice by signs to the fort below on the ships: how many, what they were, and which way they sailed". Everywhere were plants and flowers, such as wolfsbane, aloe, asphodelus, malva, prickly cedar, toadflax and Spanish broom.

Not far from Hvar was the island of Korčula, where, too, a stop was made. The island, Sir George learnt, had been taken from Ragusa by the Venetians in a very crafty way:

The Venetians had a little Island called *Saint Mark* so near to Ragusa, that it commanded the town, and yet nearer a little rock, that had no more plain ground on the top, then would be sufficient to lay the foundations of a little house. Hither, the Venetians, upon some high disgust, sent men one night, that built a little fort of past-board, painted of the colour of earth, which made it look like a strong rampart, and thereon planted wooden cannons, to the great amazement, of the towns-people next morning; which in effect put them into such a fright, that they sent presently to parley, and were glad to come off for the Island of Curzola [Korčula] in exchange of that pitiful rock. They stood for the Scoglio of St Mark also; but the Venetians would not part with that. And so they lost Curzola, which is of great use to the Venetians, who come hither often to mend and repair their vessels, the island being well covered with woods.

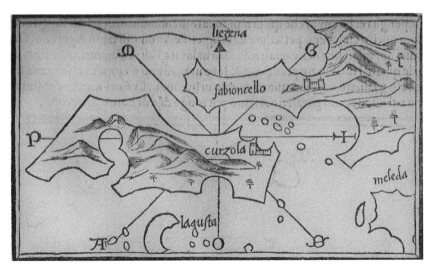

Fig. 28. Map of Korčula Island with Pelješac Peninsula (1547). Author: Bordone Benedetto. Source: Korčula City Museum. "They say that the walls of it [the city of Korčula] were built by [the emperor] Diocletian. The church's dome, dedicated to St. Mark, is an ancient edifice, and stands upon an eminence in the middle of the town, where all the streets meet."

The town's fishbone pattern of buildings served to protect the streets against the strong sunlight at noon, yet it allowed the sun in during the morning and evening. What, however, really intrigued Sir George were the island's woods, in which lived a very strange animal:

> The abundance of the woods serves for a refuge for several sorts of wild creatures, especially an animal (as they say) made like a dog; but which makes a noise like a calf or peacock. When they light any fire near the woods in the night, they hear numbers of them howl together; which make a hideous noise.

From Korčula they passed "a slip of land which makes a narrow channel between the mainland and it is, called Sabioniera" (the peninsula of Pelješac), and they approached the island of Mljet and its "Convent of Cordeliers" (a Franciscan order known under the name "Cordeliers" because of the rope they used as a belt).

Fig. 29. Myrtle blossom. Authors: Forest & Kim Starr. Source: Wikipedia CC. "All of the land was pleasantly covered with woods of myrtle-trees, that were then in the flower, and made the whole air thereabout most fragrant."

They did not stop at Ragusa, as the city was suspected to be infected with the plague. On 15 July, Castelnuovo, on the Channel of Catoro (Kotor), was sighted. It was "the first place on these coasts that belonged to the Turks". The city had been taken from Venice in 1539. Although the four thousand Spanish soldiers who had defended the city were offered safe passage to Italy and twenty ducats for each man if they abandoned their artillery and gunpowder, they refused to do so. They "preferred to die in the service of God and His Majesty", so it is said. The few who survived were flayed alive.

Il Hercule in Cunea passed Duress and they entered the Ionian Sea. Later, towards the afternoon, a ship was sighted that immediately began to flee. Thinking "them" to be pirates and reckoning on a booty, the captain of *Il Hercule in Cunea* started a pursuit "so hotly", that within less than an hour, *Il Hercule in Cunea* came "within the cannon-shot of the ship and fired two or three shots". As it happened, the ship was a merchantman from the Greek island of Cephalonia loaded with cheese and oil for Venice. Its crew had also thought *Il Hercule in Cunea* to be a pirate ship.

THE GREEK ISLANDS

Fig. 30. A map of the Greek islands. Source: Freeworldmaps.net.

The history of Greece and its islands begins with the Minoans: a people who lived on the island of Crete in the third millennium BC and who were a thriving sea power involved in trade with Egypt, Syria, Mesopotamia and Asia. Around 1500 BC, perhaps due to an earthquake and a tsunami, they disappeared. By 1100 BC, the Mycenaean civilisation on the Greek mainland had also disappeared, conquered by the Sea People from Asia. The Greek Dark Ages lasted for four hundred years.

As villages grouped together, the *polis*, or city state, was formed. At first it was ruled by a hereditary king, later by an oligarchy and sometimes by a tyrant. By the sixth century BC,

71

it was run by the *demos*, the people, and so the golden age of Ancient Greece began.

Literacy developed. On Evia (Euboea) and Crete, farming, weaving, metalworking and pottery became everyday activities. Religious and athletic festivals took place. Temples were built. And the Greeks began their massive colonisation of the Mediterranean coastal world.

In the fifth century BC, two city states dominated Greece: Athens, adventurous, open, democratic and enterprising and head of the Delian league; and Sparta, a closed society with an oligarchic government focused on its powerful military and head of the Peloponnesian league. Needless to say, they were adversaries, deadly suspicious of each other.

In 490 BC, the Persian king, Darius, invaded Greece. He was defeated at Marathon. Ten years later, the Persians returned. In Thermopylae, in a narrow passage, for three days the Spartan King, Leonidas, with 300 Spartans and 700 Thespians resisted, in the words of Herodotus, the "greatest army ever".

Freed from hostility, Greece developed democracy and a rational understanding of the world illuminated in art, philosophy and literature. Greece was the home of Socrates, Plato, Aeschylus and Aristotle. It was, too, where Hippocrates, the father of medicine, practised his skills. In Athens the dramas of Sophocles, Aeschylus and Euripides, and the comedies of Aristophanes were performed. Under Pericles (450-430 BC), the magnificent Acropolis, the Parthenon and the Propylaea were built.

But again, the old lingering animosity between Athens and Sparta emerged. It culminated with the Peloponnesian war (431-404 BC) which left Greece completely exhausted. In 338 BC, at Chaeronea, the Macedonian King, Philip II, brought Greek history to an end.

By 150 BC, Greece and its islands were under Roman rule. The Romans welcomed Greek culture, and Greek was the language of the Byzantine Empire. After the Fourth Crusade in 1204, many of the Greek islands were brought under Venetian control, and by the early sixteenth century, most of the Aegean islands had been overrun by the Ottomans.

***

Il Hercule in Cunea reached Corfu on 17 July. Anciently called Corcyra, after the daughter of the Greek river god Asopus, who was abducted by Poseidon and taken to the island, for centuries, Corfu with its invincible fort had been a "bastion of Christian faith".

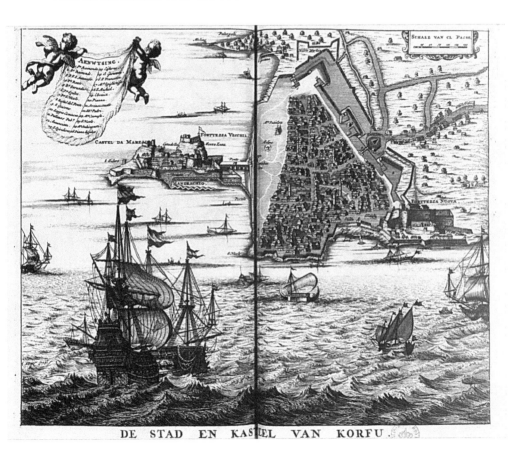

Fig. 31. A print of the fortress of Corfu (1688). Source, Wikipedia, PD. "Well provided with ammunition and artillery" and "place of residence of the Venetian generals of the Levant by sea and land".

The island was "rich in wine and oil and all sorts of good fruit", and the figs were "large and green and very delicious and refreshing in the heat of the summer". On Corfu were also many plants, especially bindweed, centaurium, licorice fern and false dittany.

Fig. 32. False dittany. Source: Landcraft Environments Ltd. "It grows in the gardens of Oxford and Paris."

Not far from the port was a little church, "famous for a picture of our lady", to which the locals attributed miracles. They would "clap a piece of money on it" and think of a friend. If the money stuck to the picture, the person was alive; if the money fell, the person was dead. Most important, however, was the sack under the picture to collect the money, so "the priest was sure of it, whether the person was dead or alive".

The ruins on Corfu belonged to the Paleopolis: an ancient metropolis with "foundations of temples, arches, pillars and marble inscriptions" and with a garden of wild olive, pear, pomegranate, apple, fig and grape vine, believed to have been that of Alcinous, "King of this place famous in Homer". The people of Corfu were said to be very vindictive:

There happened a quarrel between two families, upon no

great occasion at first; but at last was brought up to such a height that several persons were killed on both sides; especially on his side, who was the principal party offended. This man, dying, left only a young son, to whom, when he came to age several years after, it was proposed, that he should marry a daughter of his father's enemy, that so all differences might be ended, and a lasting peace made between the two families. After much solicitation he agreed to it, so that a dowry was concluded on, and married they were, with a great deal of seeming joy. But not long after, having carried his new-married wife home to his house, and having thither invited her parents, sisters, and brothers and other relations of hers, he persuaded them to stay all night, and barbarously murdered every one of them, wife and all.

Because *Il Hercule in Cunea* had to remain on the island to load cargo, Sir George and Monsieur Spon found passage to Constantinople on another ship:

They were in all six sail; whereof two men of war, and a merchant-man, were bound for Constantinople; and the other, three men of war no further than Tenos, thither to carry a new Proveditor. The General, after a very civil conference, gave us warrant to embark on the Guerriera Constante, being now informed that we were gentlemen, and that it was merely curiosity that made us so inquisitive.

Guerriera Constante's master, Zoane Bronze, was from Perasto, a town on the Bay of Kotor, Montenegro. Formerly a pirate and "for his valour well known and feared by the Turks and reverenced by the Corsairs", he was "esteemed one of the stoutest soldiers the state of Venice had in its service".

The "six sail" left Corfu on 20 July. They passed Lefkas, Ithaka and Kefalonia, which in 1570 with five-hundred ducats had been given to the Turks by Venice in exchange for Zante (Zakynthos), their next stop where they would stay for four days.

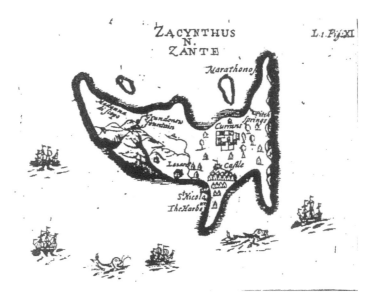

Fig. 33. Sir George Wheler's sketch of Zante. "Its good, though very strong wine, excellent oil, the best melons in the world, peaches, which were extraordinary good and big, citrons, oranges and lemons, and many springs of excellent good fresh water which rose from the ground some not above twenty paces from the sea, had earned it the title – the Golden Island."

Zante was named after the grandson of Zeus and Electra and the son of Dardanos who had founded Troy. It had some "fifty towns and villages". Because of "the frequent earthquakes which in the spring were, some years, once or twice a week and so shook all the houses, the stone walls of all of the buildings were full of great cracks".

On Zante, the raisins, so important to England, were produced:

They borrowed their name from Corinth, the famous city near the Isthmus of Morea, and are therefore called in Latin the grapes of Corinth. But none of them now grow there, being (perhaps) neglected, because they have no vend [trade] for them; the Turkish jealously permitting no great ships to enter into that gulf. They grow not upon bushes like our red and white currants, as is vulgarly thought: but upon vine like other grapes. In August, when they are ripe, they are laid thin on the ground, until they are dry: then they are gathered together, cleaned, brought into the town, and put into warehouses they call seraglio's; into which they are poured through a hole above, until the room be filled up to the top. By their own weight they cake together, that they are forced to dig them out with piked irons; and this they call stirring. When they barrel them up to send them into these parts, a man gets into the fat [currants] with bare legs and feet, and as they are brought poured in, he still keeps a stamping and treading of them down, to make them lye close together.

Why the English consumed so many raisins, the people of Zante could not know: "They were strangers to the luxury of Christmas pies, plum potage, cake and puddings".

From Zante, *Guerriera Constante* passed the Strofades where "one could not thrust a stick into the ground, but water gushed out in the place, which made them very fertile", and the islands of Sapienza, Schiza and Venetica (off the southwestern coast of the Peloponnese) which were known to be hideouts of the Barbary pirates. They plied forward and soon Cape Matapan (at the very bottom of the Peloponnese peninsula) with its city of Magna was sighted. Here, Sir George was told a story about its inhabitants – the Magnoti:

Some strangers being at one of the villages of these Magnoti, caused their baggage to be brought into an old woman's house, whilst they baited themselves, and their horses: but soon after their hostess fell bitterly a weeping. The strangers surprised at it, began to enquire the reason. Then one of them answering for her, said, that perhaps it was, because the sight of other country-men put her in mind of the miserable estate of the Magnoti were reduced unto. But she made them this short reply, and told them it was false; her weeping was because her son was not at home, to rob them of their baggage.

By 5 August they had reached their next stop – Kithira, the "native country of Venus and Helena", but which could "brag of no plenty, neither of corn, wine nor oil". In the afternoon, Sir George and Monsieur Spon went to visit Colonel Macarioti, who had retired to the island after the Ottoman siege of Candia (Crete). He offered them a very good local wine.

From Kithira, they "doubled the Cape of St Angelo". To their right was Velopoula, an extinct volcano. With a north wind they passed Falkonera, Antimilos and Milos, which was "reported to have one of the best ports in the world, but was now a refuge for the Corsairs". They approached Sifnos, "celebrated for its excellent fruits and beautiful women", and further on in the distance was Paros, "renowned for its excellent marble and anciently dedicated to Bacchus because of its plenty of wines".

By 7 August they had passed Serifos with its "convent of Greek monks dedicated to Saint Michael, the Archangel". A change of wind to the west brought them to Thermia (Kythnos), with its many baths and hot springs which were "much frequented by the paralytic, lame, and many other diseased people". They plied still northwards and passed Kea, and on 9 August they saw Tinos, the mythical residence of Aeolos, the guardian of the winds.

The "six sail" remained at Tinos for several days. The three war ships with the previous Proveditore were to return to Corfu, while *Guerriera Constante* and the two other ships would continue their voyage to Constantinople.

With time to spare, Sir George visited the island's castle (fortress). Located in the middle of the island on "the highest point of the rock, surrounded by the towns", it overlooked the whole archipelago. From the castle's tower, Sir George saw Andros, and beyond that, Evia. To the west was Kea and behind it Makronissos, "anciently Helena". And at an even greater distance was "the most southern promontory of all Attica" (Cape Sounion), while to the south was Kythnos and Serifos, and to the west was Mykonos.

There were twenty-four villages on Tinos. The people there "employed themselves in working their own silk and that of the island of Andros, and knitting stockings which they sold very cheap". The famous nearby island of Delos, the birthplace of Apollo and Artemis, however, was "utterly disinhibited" and was a "world of ruins". An Englishman – a "Signor Simon, captain of the *Saint Barbara*", Sir George was told – when visiting Delos and seeing the statue of Apollo, attempted to take it home as a souvenir. "Finding it impossible, he broke off its head, arms, and feet, and carried them with him".

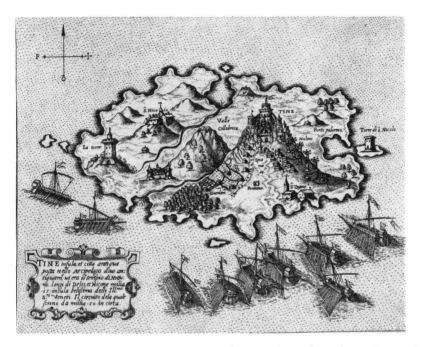

Fig. 34. Map of Tinos with the Venetian fortress (1571). Author: Giovanni Francesco Camocio. Source: Götzfried Antique Maps. "It lay high, being a large heap of marble rocks; but in many places covered with a fertile soil. It was the only island in the archipelago, that have defended themselves from the Turks; and the last in those parts under the dominion of the Venetians: with whom the inhabitants have made this agreement, viz. That when so ever they cannot, or will not protect them any longer, they shall be obliged to deliver the castle to the inhabitants; who are to have the freedom to choose whom they will for their protector."

From Tinos, the three ships headed towards the mainland and the "country of Troy". In need of fresh water, a stop was made at Mykonos.

Fig. 35. Sir George Wheler's sketch of a woman of Mykonos. "Their hair is twisted, and tied up ordinarily in a hair-lace, with pendants in their ears; over which, when they go abroad, they wrap a yellow, silken vail, as thin as tiffany, with the end flying loose about their shoulders. They wear a bodice of red or green velvet, laced with silver or gold lace in the seams; out of which come their arms, in a long and large linen sleeve, sometimes laced, or wrought at the hands, wide at the ends, resembling a surplice. About the waist is a long-plaited skirt of cloth made of cotton, under which is another garment of the same stuff plaited; which reaches down to their knees. Their legs and feet are in cotton stockings almost to the toes; which are hid with the top of their slippers, covered with velvet, sometimes laced with gold lace."

The inhabitants of this island were pirates who "here kept their wives, children, and mistresses." Captain Bronze had once kept "a seraglio (harem)" there "when he was a corsair in these seas". Later on, "being for a new game", he:

> found out a pretty young virgin for his mistress, which he bought of her brutal father, as provision for his voyage to Constantinople. Those sent by the captain went straight to

the house of this young one, who with weeping and great seeming unwillingness, suffered herself to be carried to the boat, while her mother put the rest of the women in the town in an uproar; who in multitudes followed her to the water-side. The mother stood raging on the shore, as if she had not known what her husband had done; whilst so me stood to look, and others (I judge) to be looked on: For along the shore I believe, above a hundred girls from ten or eleven, to fourteen or fifteen years old, stood with their coats as high as their middle. Thus she was conveyed aboard, and a cabin built for her, where the captain could retire to her himself, and oblige the rest of his friends.

They left Mykonos on the "Friday, the thirteenth of August". A good half of the journey had been made. "Far off, on the right hand" was Icaria, famous for the history of Icarus and Dædalus. While on the left hand, at a great distance, was Skyros, which looked like "the sails of a ship." They passed Psara and Chios where "the inhabitants cultivated the mastick and turpentine trees, and made great advantage of both of them, their gums being much valued all over Europe". And soon they saw Lesbos, where in ancient times many learned men had been born. Each of these islands, Sir George was told, paid 18,000 pieces-of-eight a year tax to the "Grand Seignior" (the Turks), while "Evia, the greatest island in the archipelago, paid a hundred thousand dollars for all its privileges".

As they neared the mainland of Troy, "the top of that famous mountain Ida, and in the same line, upon the Asian shore, the remains of a city" came into sight. Later, with a boat that was sent ashore for fresh supplies, Sir George and Monsieur Spon went to see the ruins. Everywhere were "broken pillars of marble and parts of walls and foundations none standing upright, nor whole, but lying on the ground". Perhaps they had once formed the famous city of Troy? Or perhaps they were the remains of a Roman settlement? Sir George was unsure. And here, too, were horned poppies, sea daffodil and velvet plant, the long storks of which the ancient Greeks had dipped in tallow and used as funeral torches.

On 23 August "after some days boarding against the wind", a stop was made before a "village called yet by the Greeks Troas" (the Anatolian peninsula, or Asia Minor). The inhabitants there were all Greeks "who lived by their labour, and the fruit of the ground: which consisted of corn, wine, saffron, figs, melons, almonds, and other fruits".

By 7 August they had reached Tenedos (Bozcaada, Turkey) and Imbros (Gökçeada, Turkey):

Imbros had many pleasant valleys between them, well tilled, and divided into corn-fields: and many pleasant springs of excellent water, which falling by many easy descents from the rocks, make as they pass, several pleasant little ponds to bath in, under the shade of fig-trees, wild-vines, agnus, and oleander trees.

Two days later they entered the Dardanelles (the Hellespont).

Fig. 36. The Dardanelles. Source: Paulus Swaen Old Maps & Prints. "This channel has been famous in history and has often changed name. For besides the name of Hellespont, or Sea of Hellas, daughter of Athamas,

King of Thebes, drowned in passing it, when she fled from the snares of her step-mother, Ino, it was also called the Straits of Cestos and Abydos, two cities built on each side of its banks, opposite to each other, and famous for the amours of Hero and Leander represented on some medals of those parts. And in the later times called the Dardanelli, which I believe, properly belonged to that they now call Old Castles; and by the Italians Labocca di Constantinopoli; by us the Chanel or Strait, of Constantinople."

As was the custom when entering this famous channel, Captain Bronze fired a salutation of seven guns, which was acknowledged by the Turks. He then fired a further five guns, "for at sea they still used an odd number in saluting; by which they signified they were friends".

Because of a north wind, *Guerriera Constante* and the other two ships in the convoy did not sail onto Constantinople, but remained anchored at "the New Castles" (Çanakkale and Kilitbahir). Tired of waiting, Sir George and Monsieur Spon went ashore to a nearby village to look for a boat to take them to Constantinople. Everywhere were jujube.

Fig. 37. Jujube. Source: OnePixel. "Yielding fruit, like in shape and colour to other Jujubes, but of a more meaty-taste, perhaps, because they were over-ripe."

They made stops at Gelibolu, where they learned that the plague was in the town, and "much more at Constantinople", and they passed Silivri. "All about these parts were the serraglioes, or country houses of the great men among the Turks (just as it is ten or twenty miles about London) with their gardens, vineyards and groves of cypress trees".

On 13 September, after three months at sea, Sir George was in Constantinople.

***

As Sir George Wheler saw, life along the East Adriatic and on the Greek islands was the product of centuries of Venetian domination, played out in the name of trade and profit, and more recently, subjected to a new military power in the Mediterranean – the Ottomans.

Although historically Venice was always a coloniser, its relation with the East Adriatic was not entirely exploitive. Cathedrals, churches, summer villas and even whole towns were built. On Hvar, a humanistic school taught mathematics, grammar and rhetoric and in the island's monasteries, impressive libraries were established. And, as in Venice, all of the religious holidays were celebrated with pomp. In the cities and towns of the East Adriatic, the banners of San Marco flew everywhere.

Many Dalmatians lived and worked in Venice, such as the merchants who traded in farming products, timber, valuable ores, cloths, hides, wax and other goods from their homes; the seafaring professionals who were indispensable for the Venetian galleys; the kersey trimmers, dyers and carpenters in the Arsenal; and the servants and maids in the homes of the Venetian lords. For the people of the East Adriatic, Italian was their language of commerce and literature, and the University of Padua was where they sent their sons. But perhaps the main reason why they remained so faithful to Venice was their massive fear of the Ottomans. Castelnuovo was a terrible reminder.

Differently, the Greek islands such as Scio, Lesbos, Negropont, Crete and Cyprus, once thriving economies founded on the export of wine, crops, sugar and cotton, were forgotten lands. Under the Ottomans, they were important only for the taxes they paid and were forced to pay *devshirme*: a tribute of children to be trained for the sultan's army. For the Ottomans, the pleasure-loving Greeks and their traditional spirit of liberty posed a dangerous threat to a Muslim way of life, and the ancient monuments of Greece were best broken up for stone.

Sir George Wheler never again travelled abroad. As he put it, he was "glad to return to the happiness, peace, freedom and tranquillity that we enjoy, above any nation in the world" and added:

> Enjoying some leisure in the country solitudes, I chose to retire unto, after my return, I made this and my book my divertissement.

His journey into the Levant had been an experience to last a lifetime.

CONCLUSION

Places were fundamental to the British gentleman's journey into the Levant. Places had identities. The magnificent cathedrals and churches, and the squares and buildings of the cities, were the pride of the people they served. Places were a ground to which people connected their understandings of the world. For centuries, the Holy Land had shaped the history of Europe. Places were where people created their social statuses. The stately palaces or *Ca*s of Venice, the coastal villas of Ragusa, and "the seraglios, or country houses of the great men among the Turks" of Constantinople were also built to be seen. And places were where people were involved in all sorts of social relationships and roles, as in the execution William Lithgow witnessed in St. Mark's Square:

> Mine associate and I, were no sooner landed, and perceiving a great throng of people, and in the midst of them a great smoke; but we began to demand a Venetian what the matter was? He replied, there was a grey fryer burning quick at S. Mark's pillar, of the reformed order of S. Francis, for begetting fifteen young noble nuns with child, and all within one year; he being also their farther confessor. Whereat, I sprung forward through the throng, and my friend followed me, and came just to the pillar as the half of his body and right arm fell flatling in the fire; The Friar was forty-six years old, and had been confessor of that nunnery of Sancta Lucia five years: Most of these young nuns were senators daughters; and two of them were only come in to learn virtue, and yet fell in the midst of vice.

The execution was not only about Venice's foundational values of justice and retribution: it was a stark reminder to all that nearby in the Doge's Palace were the immortal Doges and the *Consiglio dei Dieci*, the fearsome Council of Ten.

In places, people told fascinating stories. The serpent of Aleppo was surely Fynes Moryson's favourite:

> In a garden of the suburbs (of Aleppo) I did see a serpent of wonderful bigness, and they report that the male serpent and young ones, being killed by certain boys, this she serpent observing the water where the boys used to drink, did poison the same, so as many of the boys died thereof; and that the citizens thereupon came out to kill her, but seeing her lie with her face upward, as complaining to the heavens that her revenge was just, that they touched with a superstitious conceit, let her alone: finally that this serpent had lived here many ages, and was of incredible years.

But above all, places made the British gentleman think about life. If the monuments of Greece stood for a "once mistress of the civil world", they stood too, in the words of George Sandys: "… for the frailty of man, and mutability of whatsoever is worldly; and assurance that there is nothing unchangeable saving God, so nothing stable but by his grace and protection". This, we believe, was the British gentleman's message to posterity, and we'd like to pass it on.

Sources

Travelogues

Aldersey, Laurence, *The Voyage of, to the cities of Jerusalem and Tripolis, An 1581*, The Hakluyt Handbook, Vol 1, David B. Quinn (ed.) Cambridge University Press, 1974.

Austell, Henry, *The Voyage of, by Venice then to Ragusa ...* in Richard Hakluyt, *The Principal Navigations, Voyages, Traffiques and Discoveries of the English Nation*, https://archive.org/stream/principalnavigat12hakl/principalnavigat12hakl_djvu.txt.

Blout, Sir Henry, *A Voyage into the Levant*, Hard Press, 2008; https://archive.org/details/avoyageintoleva00blougoog/page/n16.

Cavendish, Harrie, *His Journey to and From Constantinople 1589 by Fox, His Servant,* Royal Historical Society, 1940, Camden 3rd series volume LXIV / 64, 1940.

Guylforde, Sir Richard, T*he pylgrymage of, to the Holy Land, A.D. 1506,* https://archive.org/details/pylgrymageofsirr00ellirich/page/n3.

Lithgow, William, *Rare Adventures & Painful Peregrinations,* Cosimo Classics, 2005.

Lok, Michael John, *The Voyage of, to Jerusalem,* in Richard Hakluyt, *The Principal Navigations.*

Moryson, Fynes, *An itinerary*, https://archive.org/details/fynesmorysons04moryuoft.

Mundy, Peter, *The travels of, in Europe and Asia*, 1608-1667, https://archive.org/details/travelspetermun00mundgoog/page/n12.

Sandys, George, https://archive.org/details/.

Watkins, Thomas, *Travels Through Switzerland, Italy, Sicily, the Greek Islands to Constantinople ...*, https://books.google.

Wey, William, *The Itineraries*, Francis Davis (ed.), The Bodleian Library, 2010.

Wheler, Sir George, *A journey into Greece by, in company of Dr. Spon of Lyons in six books* ..., http://name.umdl.umich.edu.

Further reading

Duncan-Jones, Katherine (ed.), *Philip Sidney*, Oxford University Press, 1989.

Feifer, Maxine, *Going Places*, Macmillan, 1985.

Hall, Joseph, Sparkes, *Book of the Feet*, http://www.gutenberg.org/ebooks/56978.

Mumford, Lewis, *The Culture of Cities*, A Harvest/HBJ Book.

The Travels of Sir John Mandeville, Dover Publications, Inc.